GRILLNATION

DAVID GUAS

Host of Travel Channel's *American Grilled*

GRILLNATION

200 Surefire Recipes, Tips, and Techniques to Grill Like a Pro

DAVID GUAS

Host of Travel Channel's *American Grilled*

CONTENTS

WELCOME

Truly the best thing to remember about grilling, if using a live fire or a continuous fire by gas, is that it is simple. The straightforwardness of grilling is balanced by an intriguing sense of experimentation and complexity. With a live fire, you are faced with an adventure, because the layers of heat, the hot-orange ash coal, and the flame make it unique. The pure pleasure of grilling lies in rising to these

challenges, and as the saying goes, "you live and you learn."

A grill's natural habitat is a backyard filled with loved ones. Grilling evokes feelings of comfort and togetherness in the multisensory experience it provides: The rich aromas that fill the air in wispy gray clouds of smoke; the crackling sizzle of the meat hitting the hot grill; the glossy caramelized surface of a well-marinated steak; the lush green grass padding the happy memories of summer nights gone by.

Some of my happiest memories growing up involve cooking on the grill with family, whether it was prepping hamburger meat with my mom in the kitchen; forming patties outside with my dad; learning the art of sauce making by watching my dad experiment with a pinch here and a dollop there.

There is no other cooking method as interactive and as fully absorbing as working the grill. And don't limit your cooking on the grill to only the centerpiece of the meal; you can also use it to add a smoky flavor and ineffable taste to greens, vegetables, and fruits. Be a bit more daring and intensify the meal with some extraordinary flavors that come from spending time over a flame. In this book, I share many of my dearest memories and stories, woven together with my favorite grilling recipes and basic tips. Enjoy!

David Guas

INSIDE THE GRILL

Your grill is your friend, so it's important to become acquainted with it. There are several different kinds of grills, and each kind is unique in how it functions and what kinds of grilling it can do. This quick guide explains some of the ins and outs of certain grills to help you get to know them a little bit better.

Gas Grills

PROBABLY THE MOST POPULAR type of backyard grill, the gas grill is the easiest to fire up and cook food quickly and evenly. Most gas grills involve a rectangular grate with a retractable hood and a propane tank below, hidden by cabinet-like doors. Knobs on the side control the heat, and better gas grills have multiple knobs that control different areas of the fire to allow for zoning. To cook on a gas grill, preheat all of the burners on high for 10 to 15 minutes.

There are two major disadvantages to gas grills: price and flavor. Because gas grills are meant for quick-start cooking, they involve many parts and mechanisms and tend to be much more expensive than charcoal grills. Also, though certain higher-end gas grills may come with a smoke box, a standard gas grill won't give you the depth of flavor that you can get from the smoke of different types of wood or charcoal.

Charcoal Grills

THE CHARCOAL GRILL ITSELF IS SIMPLER THAN A GAS GRILL, but the flavor it creates is more complex. Often referred to as a "kettle" grill, this portable piece of equipment is composed of a lid, a cooking grate, a round body, and legs. Due to its round design, the heat from the charcoal briquettes circulates all around the food, much like heat in an oven would.

With a little practice, the cook has much more control over the entire grilling process. You can control the heat and zoning by adding, removing, or redistributing coals; you can alter the flavor based on the type of wood or coals you choose; you can change the type of fire and smoke by selecting chips, chunks, or lumps of wood.

Charcoal grills are really for the purists. They require more time and effort than the faster gas grills, but the finished product makes it worth your while.

Kamado Grills

THE KAMADO OR CERAMIC GRILL, shaped like an urn or egg, is a well-insulated grill frequently made of ceramics or cement that, if properly maintained, can last a lifetime. It is a superb smoker and roaster—keeping meat moist and juicy because the dome shape absorbs heat and radiates it back to evenly cook foods like an oven from the top and bottom. It is easy to start in any weather because of the extraordinary insulation, and requires less charcoal than a standard grill.

However, most kamados are narrow and round so it can be difficult to properly zone the heat on them. A kettle grill works much better in that regard, allowing you to push coals to one side and move food from intense direct heat to cooler indirect heat for finishing it off. The insulation on a standard kettle grill, though, is not comparable to the quality of a kamado. Some grilling aficionados may opt to keep both around to cover all bases.

FIRE IT UP

Learn to tame the flames and grill like a pro with these helpful tips for charcoal and gas grills.

Direct Heat

Food has direct contact over the heat source. Food is turned halfway through cooking.

CHARCOAL SET-UP: Spread hot coals evenly over the bottom of kettle.

GAS SET-UP: Turn all burners to high to preheat. Place food directly on cooking grate and adjust temperature to what is recommended in the recipe.

BEST FOR: Foods that take 30 minutes or less and are less than 2 inches in thickness, such as fish, hamburgers, steak, and vegetables.

Indirect Heat

Food does not have direct contact over the heat source. Food is placed over cool side of grill and does not need to be turned.

CHARCOAL SET-UP: Bank hot coals evenly along edges of the grill; place a foil drip pan in the center of grill.

GAS SET-UP: Turn all burners to high to preheat. Turn off one burner and place food on cool side of cooking grate. Adjust temperature to what is recommended in the recipe.

BEST FOR: Foods that take longer than 30 minutes, such as large cuts of meat, whole birds, and ribs and roasts.

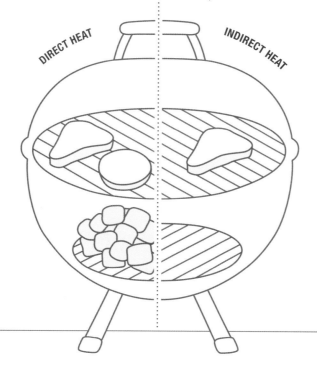

DIRECT HEAT

INDIRECT HEAT

Temperature Guide

If your grill doesn't come with a thermometer, use this chart and your trusty palm to determine the temperature. Hold your palm open over the grill and keep it there as long as you can before pulling away. The number of seconds will give you a rough estimate of heat output.

HEAT	TEMPERATURE	HAND CHECK
MEDIUM-LOW	250°F to 300°F	5 to 6 seconds
MEDIUM	300°F to 350°F	3 to 4 seconds
MEDIUM-HIGH	350°F to 400°F	2 to 3 seconds
HIGH	400°F to 500°F	1 to 2 seconds

Fire Up Your Grill with a Chimney Starter

USING A CHIMNEY STARTER IS VERY SIMPLE:

1. Following the manufacturer's instructions, stuff 1 to 2 pieces of newspaper in the bottom part of the chimney.

2. Add lump coal or charcoal briquettes through the top.

3. Light the newspaper.

The flames from the newspaper will ignite the bottom coals, which will ignite the coals above them. The concentration of the coals in a small vertical space makes a chimney starter very effective. It can light enough coals for a 22-inch kettle in about 15 minutes.

When the top coals are covered with gray ash, dump them into your grill. If you want to smoke the food while it grills, sprinkle about ½ cup wood chips on the coals.

Safety Tips

1. Follow the manufacturer's instructions.

2. Wear heat-resistant gloves.

3. Never light a chimney starter on a concrete surface (the heat may cause the concrete to crack) or on a wooden deck, dry grass, or other flammable material.

4. Remember that the starter will stay hot for awhile after you pour out the charcoal.

THE SMOKE AND NOTHING BUT THE SMOKE

Grilling with wood is one of the best ways to get the most out of open-fire cooking, providing the opportunity to add unique flavor that can't be achieved by any number of kitchen ingredients. By reducing the oxygen available to a fire, wood will smoke instead of burn, and using "green wood"—wood that isn't fully dried out—is ideal since it burns at a higher temperature and creates more smoke. With drier wood, you may need to soak it in water for 30 minutes before using it to extend its smoking life.

I really enjoy experimenting with different sizes and types of wood to see how they will affect my finished product. When you're first starting out, choosing from so many wood options can feel overwhelming, but the old adage "practice makes perfect" is certainly applicable here. To get you going, here's an overview to arm you with the basic knowledge you'll need to begin smoking on the grill.

Chips vs. Chunks vs. Logs

The first step is deciding what size pieces of wood are right for your purposes. The three basic options are: chips, chunks, and logs.

CHIPS

Chips are small shavings of wood, just a couple of inches or smaller, that both ignite and burn out quickly. They're more readily available in stores, but unless you're in a rush to get things going or can't access other wood options, you should probably skip these. You'll have to keep feeding the fire with more or use a large amount from the start.

CHUNKS

Chunks are pieces of wood usually about the size of your fist, and are the size most often used for smoking. They take longer to fully ignite than chips but burn longer on the grill—usually an hour or so—and are readily available. If you live in the city and don't have access to natural wood, you can buy reasonably priced chunks on the Internet.

LOGS

Logs are full pieces of wood like you would use in a fireplace. These generally work best in a barbecue pit but can be used on the grill if there's no other option. They'll take much longer to ignite and produce a lot more smoke than you actually need to impart the desired flavor.

Choosing your type of wood

There are six major types of wood you'll frequently see being used for smoke on the grill: cherry, apple, pecan, hickory, oak, and mesquite. Always choose a hardwood, like the abovementioned wood types. Softwoods like pine or cedar create sooty smoke that can be hazardous to your health.

Each wood carries a unique flavor, though sometimes the differences can be subtle and difficult to detect. An easier way to think about how to choose the best wood is based on the level of flavor they add. Choose **mild, medium, or heavy** depending on the protein you're cooking.

MILD

With hints of fruitiness and sweetness in the smoke, cherry and apple woods are two that I use frequently. They work well when grilling mild proteins such as fish and chicken. Cherry wood is a bit softer and sweeter than apple. I'll often turn to apple wood for pork, and sometimes I'll create wood blends with both cherry and apple to add a layer of complexity to the flavor. It's a fun way to experiment with smoke.

MEDIUM

Oak, hickory, and pecan wood fall into the medium category. Oak can be used for just about any grilled meat. (For fish, though, you'll want to stay in the mild smoke category.) Oak's flavor is stronger than fruitwood's but is lighter than hickory and pecan. It imparts a distinct smoke flavor without being overpowering. Hickory is a bit heavier, creating a stronger flavor that works well with larger cuts of meat. A nice way to keep hickory smoke balanced is by mixing it with oak or even a fruitwood, such as apple. Pecan wood is something I personally use a lot. It creates a sweet, spicy flavor that works well with beef, pork, and even chicken. Pecan wood is very popular in Louisiana so it's very familiar to me.

HEAVY

Mesquite wood falls into the heavy category and should really be reserved for certain special occasions. Mesquite is used a lot in Texas barbecue, but it's often burned down into coals before being used as a heat source. Its strength of flavor can easily overpower food. If you choose to try it, use it sparingly.

KEY EQUIPMENT AND TOOLS

Start with these key pieces of equipment for success at the grill!

1. Brass-bristle cleaning brush: Prevent proteins from sticking and avoid transferring any unwanted flavors from old burnt sauces and dripping. Brass bristles are preferable to steel because they're softer and won't damage the cooking grates.

2. Basting brush: Coat vegetables evenly with oil so the entire exterior gets that perfect crispy texture. The brush also ensures that the carefully concocted sauce you made covers every inch of meat.

3. Tongs: Tongs are a chef's best friend. Perfect for flipping and turning food, checking it for doneness, and pulling it off at just the right moment without fear of getting burned.

4. Chimney starter + newspaper: A chimney is a cylindrical canister that quickly ignites briquettes without lighter fluid.

5. Grilling spatula: Ideal for delicate pieces of fish or hearty burger patties. Choose the right weight and size spatula to give you the most control.

6. Instant-read thermometer: Easily determine the level of doneness with this trusty tool.

7. Disposable aluminum pans: In addition to making the cleanup process much easier, they are ideal for catching drips from fatty cuts of meat. They can also be filled with water to help make a moist environment for grilling ribs.

8. Grilling planks: Add flavor dimension and woodiness that varies depending on the wood used.

9. Pizza / Baking stones: Use these stones to cook pizzas, pies, pastries or breads on the grill.

10. V-Racks: Just like what you'd use for a big Thanksgiving turkey, these racks hold roasts and poultry to catch drippings, provide even roasting, and can be flipped over to serve as a rib rack.

11. Perforated grids: Great for cooking smaller foods like scallops, clams, mussels, small fish, or mushrooms that might otherwise fall through the grates.

12. Meat claws: Designed to shred big chunks of meat to get that tender, pulled result that's perfect for dishes like pulled pork sandwiches.

13. Oven mitts: Protect your hands and be sure to choose well-insulated mitts. Avoid rubber ones that may melt.

SLATHER AND SAUCE

FOOD HISTORIANS TELL US that sauces were concocted for many reasons, but there are three essential ideas why: to use as a cooking medium, as a meat tenderizer, and as a flavor enhancer. The source and inspiration for many of them vary according to culture, cuisine, or time period. Sauces teach us about where people come from. They define state lines and carry on family traditions. Sauces are passed on through generations, carrying with them longstanding family customs. In one slather, they can alter the personality of a meal. They can make things sing and dance, pop and jump. Anybody can do pork, chicken, or brisket. But it's the sauce and the rub that make it yours.

I have a profound appreciation for the power of sauces, thanks to my father, whom we proudly called "The Sauce Guy." His habit of adding various spices resulted in a batch of sauce full of different, glorious flavor each time. My wife and I have two tenacious sons with tremendous appetites who are incredibly interested in lending a hand in the kitchen. I don't know where it all goes—perhaps straight into their athletic shoes to build their stamina for baseball three times a week. Each night brings a new challenge as we repurpose the previous night's leftovers and transform them into a satisfying dinner. Our weapon of choice? Sauce, of course.

Grilled Peach BBQ
Sauce, page 23

CAROLINA MUSTARD BBQ SAUCE

MAKES 1½ cups

HANDS-ON 6 min.

TOTAL 51 min.

Mop this sweet-and-tangy sauce during the last 10 to 15 minutes of grilling.

1 cup yellow mustard	¼ cup cider vinegar
¼ cup firmly packed light brown sugar	½ tsp. kosher salt
¼ cup honey	½ tsp. coarsely ground black pepper

1. Whisk together all ingredients in a medium saucepan. Bring to a boil; reduce heat, and simmer, whisking occasionally, 15 minutes. Cool 30 minutes or to room temperature.

KANSAS CITY BBQ SAUCE

MAKES 2½ cups

HANDS-ON 1 hr., 12 min.

TOTAL 1 hr., 42 min.

This is the archetypal style of barbecue sauce, evoking the classic taste most people think of: a sweet, straight-forward sauce with hints of heat and acidity.

1 (6-oz.) can tomato paste	1 tsp. Worcestershire sauce
¾ cup light corn syrup	½ tsp. kosher salt
½ cup cider vinegar	½ tsp. garlic powder
3 Tbsp. brown sugar	½ tsp. freshly ground black pepper
3 Tbsp. dark molasses	¼ tsp. paprika

1. Whisk together all ingredients and 2 cups water in a medium saucepan. Bring to a boil over medium heat; reduce heat, and simmer, uncovered, 1 hour or until thickened, stirring occasionally. Cool 30 minutes or to room temperature. Refrigerate in an airtight container up to 1 week.

EASTERN CAROLINA VINEGAR SAUCE

MAKES 3 cups
HANDS-ON 16 min.
TOTAL 46 min.

There's something of a feud in North Carolina when it comes to barbecue sauce. Western style incorporates tomato sauce or ketchup into the mix, but Eastern doctrine dictates a strictly vinegar- and pepper-based sauce.

- 2 cups cider vinegar
- ½ cup white vinegar
- ½ cup apple juice
- 1 cup firmly packed brown sugar
- 1 Tbsp. kosher salt
- 1½ tsp. freshly ground black pepper
- ½ tsp. paprika
- ½ tsp. dried crushed red pepper

1. Whisk together all ingredients in a medium saucepan. Bring to a boil over high heat, stirring until sugar melts. Cool 30 minutes or to room temperature. Refrigerate in an airtight container up to 1 week.

ALL-PURPOSE BBQ RUB

MAKES about 1 cup
HANDS-ON 5 min.
TOTAL 5 min.

This versatile rub can be a go-to for steak, chicken, or pork.

- ¼ cup firmly packed light brown sugar
- 2 Tbsp. granulated garlic
- 2 Tbsp. kosher salt
- 2 Tbsp. coarsely ground black pepper
- 2 Tbsp. paprika
- 2 tsp. onion powder
- 1 tsp. ground cumin
- 1 tsp. dried basil
- 1 tsp. dried oregano
- 1 tsp. dried thyme

1. Stir together all ingredients in a small bowl. Store in an airtight container in a cool, dark place up to 1 month.

GRILLED PEACH BBQ SAUCE

For dessert one summer night, I served grilled peaches with a dollop of whipped mascarpone and sweet, nutty bits of pecan brittle. The fruit was charred with an irresistible color and a smoky flavor that lends itself to sauces. I refrigerated the leftovers in a sealed bag, and the next day, the peaches had macerated in their juices and created a sweet, jammy syrup. I grabbed some standard pantry staples and mixed up a surprisingly delicious barbecue sauce that is now my go-to secret recipe for the summer months.

MAKES 3 cups
HANDS-ON 43 min.
TOTAL 1 hr., 13 min.

3   medium-size ripe peaches
2   Tbsp. olive oil
½   cup diced onion
1   garlic clove
1   cup ketchup
2   Tbsp. sorghum
1   Tbsp. honey
2   Tbsp. white vinegar
1   Tbsp. dark brown sugar
¼   tsp. freshly ground black pepper

1. Light 1 side of charcoal grill or preheat gas grill to 350° to 400° (**medium-high**); leave other side unlit. Cut peaches in half; remove and discard pits. Place peaches, cut sides down, on cooking grate on lit side of grill, and grill 3 minutes. Turn peaches over, and grill, covered with grill lid, 3 more minutes. (If peaches are still firm, move them to unlit side of grill, and grill, covered with grill lid, until tender.) Remove peaches from grill; cool and chop.

2. Heat oil in a large saucepan over medium heat. Add onion and garlic, and cook 5 minutes; add chopped peaches and remaining ingredients, stirring to mix. Reduce heat to medium-low, and cook, partially covered, 30 minutes, stirring every 8 to 10 minutes.

3. Remove pan from heat; pour peach mixture into a blender, and blend 2 minutes. Cool sauce 30 minutes before serving. Refrigerate in an airtight container up to 1 week.

PRIME CHOICE

Buying produce is a sensory experience. To choose the best peaches you should rely on touch and smell. Squeeze your fruit to check that it's slightly soft, and sniff at the stem of the peach for a sweet fragrance. If you don't smell anything, the peach is not yet ripe. In case you can't find ripe peaches, make honey syrup (combine equal parts hot water and honey), pour it over halved, pitted peaches in a sealed bag, and leave for an hour or overnight. Then they're ready to grill.

PORK DRY RUB

1 cup firmly packed dark brown sugar

1 cup paprika

½ cup granulated garlic

½ cup kosher salt

2 Tbsp. dried minced onion

2 Tbsp. ground red pepper

2 Tbsp. ground chipotle chile pepper

1 Tbsp. chili powder

1 Tbsp. ground cumin

1 Tbsp. freshly ground black pepper

1 Tbsp. dry mustard

MAKES about 3½ cups
HANDS-ON 5 min.
TOTAL 5 min.

1. Stir together all ingredients in a medium bowl. Store in an airtight container in a cool, dry place up to 1 month.

SMOKY-SWEET BBQ RUB

¼ cup kosher salt

¼ cup firmly packed dark brown sugar

2 Tbsp. plus 2 tsp. smoked paprika

2 Tbsp. granulated sugar

2 tsp. garlic powder

2 tsp. freshly ground black pepper

1 tsp. dry mustard

1 tsp. ground cumin

1 tsp. ground ginger

MAKES 1 cup
HANDS-ON 5 min.
TOTAL 5 min.

1. Stir together all ingredients. Store in an airtight container in a cool, dry place up to 1 month.

COWGIRL PORK RUB

3 Tbsp. granulated garlic

2 Tbsp. kosher salt

2 tsp. light brown sugar

2 tsp. freshly ground black pepper

½ tsp. ground oregano

½ tsp. ground cumin

½ tsp. ground red pepper

MAKES about ⅓ cup
HANDS-ON 5 min.
TOTAL 5 min.

1. Stir together all ingredients. Store in an airtight container in a cool, dry place up to 1 month.

BEEF MARINADE

MAKES ⅔ cup
HANDS-ON 5 min.
TOTAL 5 min.

The soy sauce adds plenty of salt, so season the meat sparingly right before grilling.

¼ cup balsamic vinegar
2 Tbsp. soy sauce
2 Tbsp. honey

2 green onions, thinly sliced
2 tsp. chopped fresh rosemary
1½ tsp. Dijon mustard

1. Whisk together all ingredients until blended.

SWEET-AND-SPICY MARINADE

MAKES 2⅔ cups
HANDS-ON 8 min.
TOTAL 8 min.

The flavors mellow as this mixture stands, so make it a few hours before you plan to grill.

1 cup ketchup
⅔ cup firmly packed brown sugar
½ cup orange juice

⅓ cup Dijon mustard
1 Tbsp. Worcestershire sauce
1 Tbsp. balsamic vinegar
2 tsp. dried crushed red pepper

1. Whisk together all ingredients in a medium saucepan. Bring to a boil, and cook, whisking occasionally, 5 minutes. Cool completely.

ASIAN SEAFOOD MARINADE

MAKES about ¾ cup
HANDS-ON 15 min.
TOTAL 15 min.

This marinade makes enough for about 2 pounds of fish or seafood.

⅓ cup dark sesame oil
¼ cup fresh lime juice
1 Tbsp. brown sugar
3 Tbsp. mirin (sweet rice wine)
3 Tbsp. soy sauce

1 tsp. minced garlic
½ tsp. toasted sesame seeds
½ tsp. freshly ground black pepper
¼ tsp. dried crushed red pepper

1. Whisk together all ingredients until blended.

COAL-ROASTED GARLIC COMPOUND BUTTER

MAKES ½ cup
HANDS-ON 5 min.
TOTAL 1 hr., 20 min.

Linton Hopkins (chef/owner of Restaurant Eugene and Holeman and Finch, Atlanta) and I worked and lived together in New Orleans. One night off the line, Linton prepared rib-eye steaks with Rapini, and the first thing he did was slice the top off two heads of garlic and roast them in a cast-iron skillet with a touch of chicken stock, olive oil, salt, and pepper. The garlic came out soft and succulently sweet, and we squeezed it all over the meal. I never looked back and made that technique a customary process in my home and professional kitchen. When I'm grilling, I'll wrap the garlic in foil and cook it directly in the coals. A garlic compound butter that melts into the steak makes you pause long enough to savor every bite.

1   garlic bulb
1   Tbsp. olive oil
     Coarse sea salt
     Freshly ground black pepper
½   cup unsalted butter, softened
     Parchment paper or plastic wrap

1. Light charcoal grill or preheat gas grill to 350° to 400° (**medium-high**). Cut off and discard top of garlic bulb. Place garlic bulb in center of a 12-inch piece of aluminum foil; pull up edges of foil to form a bowl. Drizzle oil over bulb, and season with salt and pepper to taste. Add ¼ cup water, and double fold top edge of foil to seal, making a packet.

2. Place packet directly on briquettes or on grill grate, with briquettes along the edges but not on top of packet; cover with grill lid, and grill for 1 hour. Remove packet from grill; carefully open packet with tongs to avoid being burned by hot steam. Cool for 15 minutes.

3. Place butter in a small bowl, and squeeze each clove over butter, discarding skins; mix well. Place mixture on parchment paper or plastic wrap, and roll up to form a log. Refrigerate up to 3 days, or freeze up to 3 months.

CHARRED JALAPEÑO-HONEY BUTTER

MAKES 1 cup
HANDS-ON 5 min.
TOTAL 25 min.

2	medium jalapeño peppers	3	Tbsp. wildflower honey
1	cup unsalted butter, softened	½	tsp. kosher salt

1. Light charcoal grill or preheat gas grill to 350° to 400° (**medium-high**). Place peppers on the cooking grate, and grill for 5 minutes or until charred, turning frequently. Remove from grill; cool 15 minutes.

2. Cut peppers lengthwise; remove seeds, and finely chop. Combine butter, honey, and salt in a mixing bowl, and mix well; stir in chopped peppers. Refrigerate in an airtight container up to 2 weeks, or freeze up to 2 months.

WHITE BBQ SAUCE

MAKES 1⅔ cups
HANDS-ON 5 min.
TOTAL 5 min.

1	cup mayonnaise	½	tsp. garlic powder
⅓	cup apple cider vinegar	½	tsp. onion powder
1	tsp. Worcestershire sauce	½	tsp. freshly ground black pepper
½	tsp. kosher salt	¼	tsp. hot sauce

1. Stir together all ingredients and 3 teaspoons water in a small bowl. Serve immediately, or cover and chill. Refrigerate in an airtight container up to 3 days.

VIDALIA ONION & PEACH REFRIGERATOR RELISH

MAKES about 10 (8-oz.) jars
HANDS-ON 25 min.
TOTAL 1 hr., 25 min.

2	cups sugar	½	tsp. dried crushed red pepper
2	cups cider vinegar	4	bay leaves, crushed
¼	cup gin	3	lb. Vidalia onions, finely chopped
2	Tbsp. table salt		
1	Tbsp. mustard seeds	3	lb. fresh peaches, peeled and chopped
1	tsp. celery salt	4	garlic cloves, thinly sliced

1. Bring 2 cups water, sugar, and next 7 ingredients to a boil in a Dutch oven over medium-high heat. Add onions, peaches, and garlic; boil, stirring occasionally, 15 minutes. Cool mixture completely (about 2 hours). Refrigerate in airtight containers up to 2 weeks.

Charred Jalapeño-
Honey Butter

Cowboy Cast-Iron
Cornbread, page 52

GRILLED SMOKED VIDALIA ONION MARMALADE

One afternoon when I had the grill ripping wicked hot, I walked into my kitchen and saw a bowl of Vidalia onions—the only kind I buy when they're in season because of their sweet Georgia flavor. They were just staring at me, and I knew they'd make a perfect onion marmalade. This recipe is rich in complexity, with Southern smoke from the pecan wood, a slight char from the grill, and a bit of texture from the whole mustard seeds. It is a marriage of perfection on a beer-boiled hot dog with some good grainy mustard.

MAKES about 3 cups
HANDS-ON 22 min.
TOTAL 1 hr., 45 min.

Wood chips

3 Vidalia or other sweet onions, cut into ¼-inch slices

1 Tbsp. mustard seeds

¼ cup light brown sugar

¼ cup apple cider vinegar

¼ cup cane syrup

1. Light 1 side of charcoal grill or preheat gas grill to 350° to 400° (**medium-high**); leave other side unlit. Meanwhile, soak wood chips in water 30 minutes. Spread wood chips on a large sheet of heavy-duty aluminum foil; fold edges to seal. Poke several holes in top of pouch with a fork. Place pouch directly on lit side of grill; cover with grill lid.

2. Place onions in heat-proof pan. Place pan over unlit side of grill, and smoke, covered with grill lid, 20 to 25 minutes. Remove pan from grill, and let stand 10 minutes.

3. Heat the mustard seeds in a saucepan over medium-low heat, stirring often, 2 minutes or until the seeds begin to dance and turn brown. Add onions, sugar, vinegar, and syrup; stir to mix. Increase heat to medium-high, and cook, covered and stirring occasionally, 15 minutes. Reduce heat to medium; cook, uncovered, 30 minutes or until most of the liquid evaporates. Refrigerate in an airtight container up to 2 weeks, or freeze up to 3 months.

David's
TIPS

"Pork up" this recipe by rendering some chopped bacon in the pan first. Add the cooked bacon at the end.

STARTERS AND SNACKS

LIFE IS ALL ABOUT FIRST IMPRESSIONS, and meals are no exception. Imagine your guests patiently waiting at the dining table and the savory aromas wafting in from the kitchen. Out comes a platter of crostini—crusty and tangy sourdough bread beautifully marked with a mahogany color, some dripping in garlicky Caesar dressing and grilled romaine, and some topped with Gorgonzola cheese and crisp pear slices. An outstanding starter opens diners' minds and mouths for the supper to come, or for a tasty in-between meal tease. The first course introduces your culinary personality and the rest just naturally follows suit.

As a professionally trained cook I'm used to the luxuries of a big, sleek stainless steel convection oven that has perfectly controlled temperatures. It changes the whole playing field when taking meals outdoors to an open flame. Nothing gives me more pleasure than a long ride on my Harley Davidson Softail Deuce Motorcycle, getting out of the city on the open road to a remote place. One particular afternoon, a few riding buddies and I ventured to Hackenberg Apiaries in Lewisburg, Pennsylvania, where I get most of the honey used at my restaurant Bayou Bakery, Coffee Bar & Eatery. Surrounded by lush greenery and armed with fresh honey and my trusty cast-iron skillet, I dug a fire pit. Channeling my inner Boy Scout, I built a fire with coal and wood sticks. I mixed up a gritty cornbread batter, wrapped my skillet in foil, and nestled it into the coals to create a make-shift Dutch oven. The end result was a rustic cornbread snack, cooked slightly unevenly but chockfull of sweet, savory, smoky flavor and lots of personality.

Grilled Caesar
Crostini, page 39

PORK TENDERLOIN CROSTINI

MAKES 4 dozen
HANDS-ON 30 min.
TOTAL 2 hr., 50 min.

Pork tenderloin should be served slightly pink in the center.

24 frozen tea biscuits
2 (¾- to 1-lb.) pork tenderloins
2 Tbsp. olive oil
1 tsp. table salt
2 tsp. freshly ground black pepper
5 Tbsp. butter, melted
  Cranberry-Pepper Jelly
1 bunch fresh watercress

1. Preheat oven to 350°. Bake tea biscuits according to package directions. Cool on a wire rack 20 minutes.

2. Light charcoal grill or preheat gas grill to 350° to 400° (**medium-high**). Remove silver skin from each tenderloin; rub with oil, and sprinkle with salt and pepper. Grill tenderloins, covered with grill lid, 10 to 12 minutes on each side or until a meat thermometer inserted into thickest portion registers 145°. Remove from grill; cover with aluminum foil, and let stand 15 minutes.

3. Meanwhile, cut biscuits in half; brush cut sides with butter; arrange, cut sides up, on a baking sheet. Bake at 350° for 8 to 10 minutes or until edges are golden.

4. Cut tenderloins into ¼-inch-thick slices. Place on biscuits; top with Cranberry-Pepper Jelly and watercress. Serve immediately.

CRANBERRY-PEPPER JELLY

Makes: 3 cups Hands-on: 25 min. Total: 1 hr., 10 min.

1 (12-oz.) package fresh cranberries
1 (10-oz.) jar red pepper jelly
1½ cups peeled and diced Granny Smith apple
¾ cup sugar
¼ tsp. dried crushed red pepper
½ cup sweetened dried cranberries

1. Bring first 5 ingredients and ½ cup water to a boil in a large saucepan over medium-high heat, stirring often. Reduce heat to medium-low, and simmer, stirring often, 10 to 15 minutes or until cranberries begin to pop and mixture starts to thicken.

2. Remove from heat; stir in sweetened dried cranberries. Cool completely (about 45 minutes). Serve at room temperature, or cover and chill before serving. Refrigerate in an airtight container up to 2 weeks.

GRILLED CAESAR CROSTINI

This recipe was inspired by one of my favorite snacks as a kid. In my younger years, I used to pour some croutons into a bowl, drizzle them with Caesar dressing, and eat them like cereal. That savory crunch, that salty anchovy flavor, that creamy topping—what could be better? Now my boys love anything involving anchovies, too, so I try to find creative ways to incorporate them into meals. These crostini are always a home run.

SERVES 6
HANDS-ON 14 min
TOTAL 14 min.

3   cloves garlic
1   tsp. Dijon mustard
2   Tbsp. lemon juice
¼   tsp. freshly ground black pepper
¼   tsp. kosher salt
1   tsp. hot sauce
1   tsp. Worcestershire sauce
2   egg yolks

3   anchovy fillets
½   cup vegetable oil
½   rustic bread loaf, sliced diagonally into ½-inch-thick slices
3   Tbsp. extra virgin olive oil
    Kosher salt
1   romaine lettuce heart
2   ounces Parmesan cheese, peeled into large curls

1. Light charcoal grill or preheat gas grill to 350° to 400° (**medium-high**). Place garlic and next 8 ingredients in a blender. Turn blender on high; gradually add ½ cup vegetable oil in a slow, steady stream. Refrigerate in an airtight container until ready to use.

2. Brush each slice of bread with olive oil, reserving any remaining olive oil; sprinkle with salt. Place on cooking grate, and grill until grill marks appear and bread is well toasted.

3. Meanwhile, cut lettuce into pieces, and drizzle with remaining olive oil; place, cut sides down, on cooking grate. Grill, turning occasionally, 1 to 2 minutes or until charred. Remove lettuce from grill, and shred.

4. Drizzle dressing over toasted bread slices, and top evenly with shredded romaine. Drizzle with additional dressing, and sprinkle evenly with Parmesan cheese curls.

David's TIPS

When grilling the bread, don't walk away from the grill. You just want to crisp the outside for about 45 seconds and then pull it off the heat. The idea is to maintain the integrity of the center of the bread— the soft center makes these much easier to chew.

TOMATO BRUSCHETTA

SERVES 8
HANDS-ON 17 min.
TOTAL 17 min.

Make this bruschetta mixture up to 4 hours ahead of time, but be sure to drain it before using.

16 (½-inch-thick) slices French bread baguette
3   Tbsp. extra virgin olive oil
4   ripe tomatoes, seeded and chopped
½   small sweet onion, thinly sliced
½   cup torn fresh basil
1   garlic clove, minced
½   tsp. kosher salt
¼   tsp. freshly ground black pepper

1. Light charcoal grill or preheat gas grill to 350° to 400° (**medium-high**). Brush both sides of bread slices with oil. Grill 1 to 1½ minutes per side or until toasted.

2. Toss together tomatoes and next 5 ingredients; serve over bread slices.

GORGONZOLA-GRILLED PEAR CROSTINI

MAKES 3 dozen
HANDS-ON 22 min.
TOTAL 22 min.

Salty, creamy Gorgonzola is an excellent cheese to pair with fragrant, crisp fruit like pears. This crunchy crostini is the perfect bite to open the way to a delicious meal.

3 firm, ripe Bartlett pears, cut into ¼-inch-thick wedges
½ (8-oz.) package cream cheese, softened
4 oz. Gorgonzola cheese, crumbled
¼ cup butter, softened
2 Tbsp. dry sherry
36 French bread baguette slices, toasted
½ cup finely chopped, lightly salted roasted pecans
2 Tbsp. finely chopped fresh rosemary
¼ cup honey

1. Light charcoal grill or preheat gas grill to 350° to 400° (**medium-high**). Grill pear wedges, covered with grill lid, 1 to 2 minutes on each side or until golden.

2. Stir together cream cheese and next 3 ingredients; spread about ½ Tbsp. on each bread slice. Top with grilled pears; sprinkle with pecans and rosemary, and drizzle with honey.

CHARRED GUACAMOLE WITH GRILLED CORN

Although this tasty mixture makes the perfect sidekick for tortilla chips, it is equally delicious piled on top of grilled chicken or steak.

MAKES 3¼ cups
HANDS-ON 23 min.
TOTAL 50 min.

2 ears fresh corn, husks removed

1 small red onion, cut into ½-inch-thick slices

3 avocados, halved

2 Tbsp. olive oil

1¼ tsp. Pork Dry Rub (page 25), divided

¼ cup chopped fresh cilantro

¼ cup fresh lime juice

2 garlic cloves, minced

1. Light charcoal grill or preheat gas grill to 350° to 400° (**medium-high**). Brush corn, onion slices, and cut sides of avocados with oil; sprinkle with 1 tsp. rub. Grill corn, covered with grill lid, 12 minutes or until done, turning occasionally. At the same time, grill onion slices, covered with grill lid, 4 minutes on each side. Grill avocados, cut sides down, covered with grill lid, 3 minutes. Remove from grill; cool 15 minutes.

2. Stir together remaining ¼ tsp. rub, cilantro, lime juice, and garlic in a medium bowl. Hold each ear of corn upright on a cutting board; carefully cut downward, cutting kernels from cob. Add kernels to cilantro mixture, and discard cobs; chop onion and avocados, and add to mixture. Mash mixture with a fork or potato masher just until chunky. Serve immediately.

STEP-BY-STEP

1. Use a basting brush to oil the vegetables directly on the grill.

2. Don't overwork the avocado. Mash mixture with a fork just until it is chunky.

3. Serve in a decorative bowl with plenty of tortilla chips.

Chipotle-Mango Salsa

GRILLED SALSA

2 ears fresh corn, husks removed

1 small sweet onion, cut into ¼-inch-thick slices

6 medium tomatoes, halved (about 2 lb.)

½ jalapeño pepper, seeded (optional)

Vegetable cooking spray

1 small garlic clove, quartered

¼ cup loosely packed fresh cilantro leaves

2 Tbsp. fresh lime juice

1½ tsp. table salt

MAKES 4 cups
HANDS-ON 30 min.
TOTAL 45 min.

1. Light charcoal grill or preheat gas grill to 350° to 400° (**medium-high**). Coat corn, onion slices, cut sides of tomatoes, and jalapeño pepper, if desired, lightly with cooking spray. Grill corn and onion slices, covered with grill lid, 15 minutes or until golden brown, turning occasionally. At the same time, grill tomatoes and jalapeño pepper, covered with grill lid, 8 minutes or until grill marks appear, turning occasionally.

2. Remove from grill, and cool 15 minutes. Hold each ear of corn upright on a cutting board; carefully cut downward, cutting kernels from cob; discard cobs. Coarsely chop onion. Pulse garlic and next 2 ingredients in a food processor until finely chopped. Add grilled tomatoes, onion, and jalapeño pepper to food processor, in batches, and pulse after each addition until well blended; transfer to a large bowl. Stir in salt and corn. Serve immediately.

CHIPOTLE-MANGO SALSA

1¼ cups peeled and chopped mango

⅓ cup chopped red onion

⅓ cup chopped red bell pepper

⅓ cup fresh lime juice

2 Tbsp. honey

¼ cup chopped fresh cilantro

1 Tbsp. minced canned chipotle pepper in adobo sauce

1 tsp. kosher salt

¼ tsp. coarsely ground black pepper

2 garlic cloves, minced

MAKES 2 cups
HANDS-ON 25 min.
TOTAL 25 min.

1. Stir together all ingredients in a medium bowl. Cover and chill until ready to serve.

GRILLED OYSTERS WITH SPICY COCKTAIL SAUCE

Serve any remaining cocktail sauce with boiled shrimp or your favorite seafood.

MAKES 2 dozen
HANDS-ON 25 min.
TOTAL 25 min.

2 dozen fresh oysters in the shell
   Spicy Cocktail Sauce

1. Light charcoal grill or preheat gas grill to 300° to 350° (**medium**). Place oysters in a single layer on grill grate.

2. Grill oysters, covered with grill lid, 20 minutes or until oysters open. Serve with Spicy Cocktail Sauce.

SPICY COCKTAIL SAUCE

Makes: about 4 cups Hands-on: 10 min. Total: 10 min.

1½ cups chili sauce

1 cup ketchup

¾ cup refrigerated horseradish

⅓ cup fresh lemon juice

1½ Tbsp. Worcestershire sauce

2 to 3 tsp. hot sauce

½ tsp. table salt

½ tsp. freshly ground black pepper

1. Stir together all ingredients until blended. Cover and chill until ready to serve.

STEP-BY-STEP

1. Purchase oysters that have been stored directly on ice.

2. If any of the oysters do not open during grilling, discard and do not eat.

GRILLED SAUSAGE SALAD PIZZA

SERVES 6

HANDS-ON 45 min.

TOTAL 45 min.

Add a kick to this pizza by swapping out smoked sausage for hot Italian sausage.

1   medium-size sweet onion, cut into ¼-inch-thick slices
3   Tbsp. olive oil, divided
½   lb. smoked link sausage
1   (16-oz.) package prebaked Italian pizza crust
1½ cups (6 oz.) freshly shredded mozzarella cheese
1¼ tsp. kosher salt, divided
1   cup firmly packed arugula
½   cup fresh flat-leaf parsley
½   tsp. freshly ground black pepper
1   lemon, halved

1. Light charcoal grill or preheat gas grill to 350° to 400° (**medium-high**). Brush onion slices with 1 Tbsp. oil; grill onion, covered with grill lid, 6 minutes on each side. Grill sausage 4 minutes on each side; slice.

2. Brush pizza crust with 1 Tbsp. oil; grill, oil side down, 2 minutes. Turn crust over, and brush with remaining 1 Tbsp. oil; sprinkle with cheese and ¼ tsp. salt. Grill 2 minutes or until cheese melts.

3. Toss together arugula, parsley, pepper, sausage slices, onion slices, and remaining 1 tsp. salt. Top pizza with salad; squeeze lemon juice over top. Serve immediately.

GRILLED TOMATO-PEACH PIZZA

SERVES 4
HANDS-ON 20 min.
TOTAL 26 min.

If you are having trouble rolling out the pizza dough, place the dough in the refrigerator for 10 minutes to relax the gluten.

Vegetable cooking spray
2   tomatoes, sliced
½   tsp. table salt
1   large peach, peeled and sliced
1   lb. bakery pizza dough, at room temperature
½   (16-oz.) package fresh mozzarella, sliced
4   to 6 fresh basil leaves
     Garnishes: coarsely ground black pepper, olive oil

1. Coat cold cooking grate with cooking spray, and place on grill. Light charcoal grill or preheat gas grill to 300° to 350° (**medium**).

2. Sprinkle tomatoes with salt; let stand 15 minutes. Pat tomatoes dry with paper towels.

3. Grill peach slices, covered with grill lid, 2 to 3 minutes on each side or until grill marks appear.

4. Place dough on a large baking sheet coated with cooking spray; lightly coat dough with cooking spray. Roll dough to ¼-inch thickness (about 14 inches in diameter). Slide pizza dough from baking sheet onto cooking grate.

5. Grill, covered with grill lid, 2 to 3 minutes or until lightly browned; reduce grill temperature to 250° to 300° (**low**). Turn dough over, and top with tomatoes, grilled peaches, and mozzarella. Grill, covered with grill lid, 5 minutes or until cheese melts. Arrange basil leaves over pizza. Serve immediately.

GRILLED PORTOBELLO PIZZA

½ cup finely chopped fresh basil

2 tsp. olive oil

1 tsp. bottled minced roasted garlic

12 plum tomatoes, seeded and chopped

1½ Tbsp. minced fresh thyme

1 tsp. olive oil

1 Tbsp. bottled minced roasted garlic

4 (4-inch) portobello mushroom caps
 Vegetable cooking spray

¼ tsp. table salt

¼ tsp. freshly ground black pepper

½ cup (2 oz.) shredded part-skim mozzarella cheese

SERVES 4
HANDS-ON 15 min.
TOTAL 23 min.

1. Combine first 3 ingredients in a small bowl; stir well, and set aside. Combine tomato and next 3 ingredients in a medium bowl; stir well, and set aside.

2. Remove brown gills from the undersides of mushrooms with a spoon; discard gills. Coat top and bottom of mushroom caps evenly with cooking spray; sprinkle with salt and pepper.

3. Coat grill rack with cooking spray. Light charcoal grill or preheat gas grill to 300° to 350° (**medium**). Place mushrooms, top side up, on rack; grill, covered, 4 minutes. Turn mushrooms over; spoon tomato mixture evenly into caps; top each mushroom with 1 tablespoon basil mixture and 2 tablespoons cheese. Grill, covered, 4 minutes or until mushrooms are tender and cheese melts.

COWBOY CAST-IRON CORNBREAD

SERVES 12
HANDS-ON 10 min.
TOTAL 1 hr.

Just sayin'—I love cornbread. It may be considered a Lowcountry favorite that you'd find in Charleston, but it was certainly on our dining table in New Orleans. Cornbread can range from soft and sweet to coarse and savory, or some combination in between. Some folks don't like to add any sugar and instead add fresh corn for sweetness. Others use corn flour and sugar to basically make a cake. Me? I like to add a little sugar to complement the natural sweetness of the corn, but I add plenty of salt for balance.

7	oz. all-purpose flour	6	oz. sour cream
4	oz. cornmeal	⅓	cup milk
3	oz. sugar	½	cup plus 3 Tbsp. peanut oil
2	tsp. kosher salt	3	oz. creamed corn
2	tsp. baking powder	5	Tbsp. butter, melted
1	large egg		Charred Jalapeno-Honey Butter (page 30)

1. Create a small fire in an open area with gray coals or preheat gas grill to 350° to 400° (**medium-high**).

2. In a mixing bowl, combine flour, cornmeal, sugar, salt, and baking powder. Add egg, sour cream, milk, ½ cup oil, and creamed corn. With a wooden spoon, stir together until combined. Add melted butter, and stir until combined.

3. Coat a 10-inch (4 inches deep) cast-iron pot with the remaining 3 Tbsp. oil. Place lid on pot, and place near the coals for 8 to 10 minutes to allow the pot to heat up. Pour batter into the cast-iron pot. Cover the pot with lid, and make sure it is well sealed. Place the pot in the center of the fire, directly on the ground with the gray coals around but not touching the sides of the pot (leave about 4 inches of space between the coals and pot). Sprinkle some of the coals directly on the top of the lid and cook for about 45 minutes to an hour (if baking on a gas grill, close lid). Check the cornbread every 15 minutes, as cooking times will vary due to the use of a campfire. Rotate pot, and make sure coals are always smoldering around the pot.

4. Remove pot from grilling area, and allow to cool 5 minutes. Slice and serve with Charred Jalapeño-Honey Butter (page 30).

David's
TIPS

If you don't have a Dutch oven at home, this recipe can be made in a cast-iron skillet or another deep, heavy-bottomed pan on the grill. Just be sure to cover it with a lid.

COUNTRY BOY ON THE ROCKS

From the way the heat releases those pulpy juices to the stunning aesthetic appeal when it gets that nice char, citrus is an unsung hero of the grill—but it often gets forgotten. This cocktail is the house drink of choice for any shindig spontaneously put together in my backyard. The grilled lemon slices add just the right amount of acidity to this simple combination.

SERVES 8
HANDS-ON 5 min.
TOTAL 5 min.

2   qts. unsweetened tea

1   qt. lemonade

2   lemons

8   (16-oz.) Mason jars

1   (750-ml.) bottle bourbon

1   bunch fresh mint

1. Combine tea and lemonade in a large container; cover and chill.

2. Cut lemons into 8 slices. Light charcoal grill or preheat gas grill to 400° to 500° (**high**). Grill lemon slices, covered with grill lid, 3 to 5 minutes or until charred.

3. For each serving, place ice in a Mason jar, filling ⅔ full. Add ¼ cup bourbon, and fill jar with tea-lemonade mixture. Pour drink into a shaker, and add 3 to 4 mint leaves and 1 slice charred lemon; cover and shake 10 seconds. Pour mixed drink back into jar; add more ice, if desired.

David's TIPS

For an even more authentic Southern cocktail, you can make your own sun tea. Fill a pitcher with water, and add bags of Luzianne tea or other good black tea. Leave it out in the sun for one day to steep.

CUCUMBER GIN AND TONIC

MAKES 4 cups
HANDS-ON 5 min.
TOTAL 1 hr., 35 min.

4 Kirby cucumbers, divided
3 limes, divided
2 cups gin
½ cup tonic concentrate
Ice cubes
2 cups chilled club soda

1. Cut 3 Kirby cucumbers into ½-inch-thick slices and 2 limes into 6 wedges; muddle in a bowl to release flavors. Stir in gin and tonic concentrate; let stand 30 minutes. Using back of a spoon, press mixture through a fine wire-mesh strainer into a large container; discard solids. Cover and chill 1 to 2 hours.

2. Cut remaining Kirby cucumber and remaining lime into ¼-inch-thick slices. Fill a large pitcher with ice cubes; add cucumber and lime slices. Stir in gin mixture and chilled club soda.

TOMATO-TEQUILA FIZZ

MAKES 6 cups
HANDS-ON 5 min
TOTAL 1 hr., 20 min.

1 cup grape tomato halves, divided
¼ cup loosely packed mint leaves
1 lime, cut into wedges
¼ tsp. kosher salt
2 cups tequila
¼ cup light agave nectar
Ice cubes
Fresh mint sprigs
4 cups chilled club soda

1. Muddle ¾ cup grape tomato halves, ¼ cup loosely packed mint leaves, lime wedges, and salt in a medium bowl to release flavors. Stir in tequila and agave nectar; let stand 15 minutes. Using back of a spoon, press mixture through a fine wire-mesh strainer into a large container; discard solids. Cover and chill 1 to 2 hours.

2. Fill a large pitcher with ice cubes; add remaining ¼ cup grape tomato halves and fresh mint sprigs. Add chilled tomato mixture and chilled club soda. Stir gently.

BACKYARD NOLA SWINGERS

This drink was motivated by a visit from my friend Lolis Eric Elie, who knows just about all there is to know about New Orleans and its rich history and culture. In his cookbook, *Treme: Stories and Recipes from the Heart of New Orleans,* he includes a recipe with a grapefruit and honey base called N'awlins Nectar. When I hosted him at Bayou Bakery, I used his base idea and jazzed it up a bit with fresh rosemary and jalapeños to give it that NOLA spice.

SERVES 8
HANDS-ON 5 min.
TOTAL 1 hr., 5 min.

2   cups wildflower honey
2   qts. grapefruit juice
8   (16-oz.) Mason jars
1   (750-ml.) bottle dark rum
8   fresh rosemary sprigs
1   medium jalapeño pepper, thinly sliced

1. Stir together honey and ¾ cup water in a large container. Add grapefruit juice, and stir well; cover and chill about 1 hour.

2. For each serving, place ice in a Mason jar, filling ⅔ full. Add ¼ cup rum, and fill jar with grapefruit juice mixture. Pour drink into a shaker, and add 1 sprig rosemary and 1 slice jalapeño pepper; cover and shake 10 seconds. Pour mixed drink back into jar; add more ice, if desired.

David's
TIPS

Kermit Ruffins is one of my favorite jazz musicians—he's also the best trumpet player in the Tremé neighborhood of New Orleans. He and his band, the Barbecue Swingers, sing a lot about the beloved pastime of backyard grilling, which inspired the name for this drink.

BURGERS AND BRATS

AS A YOUNG BOY, I remember rushing home after school to watch one of best TV shows on the planet, *Happy Days.* I was instantly drawn to the beacon of all burger joints, Arnold's Drive-In, and all that it represented. I wanted my parents to take me there so I, too, could experience the grill-top aroma of its infamous burgers, French fries, and onion rings served at the side of our family car. These days, burger joints continue to be insanely popular, from the grungy neighborhood spot to the gourmet pop-up. They are truly one of the quintessential symbols of America, just like apple pie and Chevrolet.

Plain and simple, burgers are my mom's single most favorite food. Whenever she and I were together in the car with even the slightest appetite, we couldn't resist stopping by Bud's Broiler for a double patty with Cheddar, onions, and the signature hickory smoked sauce. The sharp Cheddar was grated on top in a thick layer that didn't fully melt, and it was dangerously good. Oh, and that sauce! It was the real deal—smoky, tangy, sweet perfection. That was our sacred time together. Burgers take me back to my oldest memory of grilling. The ground meat was seasoned liberally with Tony Chachere's Creole Seasoning—a staple condiment in any New Orleans kitchen and one that I still always keep on hand in my pantry.

And don't forget the dogs! My dad's big thing was beer-boiled dogs—soaked in beer for a few hours then tossed on the grill to finish. In this chapter, you'll find my favorite burgers and brats. Experiment with your favorite toppings to make new memories of your own.

The Beefy Burger,
page 71

SERRANO PEPPER BURGERS

SERVES 12
HANDS-ON 30 min.
TOTAL 45 min.

Serrano peppers can be quite hot, so if you are a little timid, substitute a milder pepper such as a red Fresno.

1 lb. serrano peppers
2 Tbsp. olive oil
   Kosher salt
3 lb. ground chuck
   Freshly ground black pepper
1 lb. pepper Jack cheese, thinly sliced
   Butter
12 hamburger buns
   Toppings: mayonnaise, ketchup, mustard, lettuce leaves, tomato slices

1. Light 1 side of charcoal grill or preheat gas grill to 350° to 400° (**medium-high**); leave other side unlit. Toss together peppers and oil. Arrange peppers in a grill basket or on an aluminum foil tray over unlit side; grill, covered with grill lid, 10 to 15 minutes or until peppers begin to shrivel. Transfer peppers to lit side of grill, and grill, covered with grill lid, 8 to 10 minutes or until lightly charred, turning after 4 minutes. Remove from grill to a wire rack, and cool completely (about 15 minutes). Remove and discard stems; slice peppers in half lengthwise. Remove seeds, and sprinkle peppers with desired amount of salt.

2. Light other side of grill, and preheat to 350° to 400° (**medium-high**). Shape ground chuck into 12 patties; sprinkle with desired amount of salt and pepper. Grill patties, without grill lid, 4 to 5 minutes on each side or until desired degree of doneness. Place 2 to 3 pepper halves on each patty; top with cheese. Grill, covered with grill lid, 1 to 2 minutes or until cheese melts.

3. Butter inside of each bun, and toast on grill. Serve burgers on toasted buns with desired toppings.

David's TIPS

When using tongs, watch out for cross contamination since your tongs come in contact with raw meat. I recommend buying two pairs of tongs and marking them "raw" and "cooked," to ensure that you do not use the same one twice.

PINEAPPLE-JALAPEÑO BURGERS

Crank up the heat on this fun burger combo by adding finely chopped jalapeño into the meat mixture itself. The added spice tastes great with the caramelized grilled pineapple slice and the jalapeño cream sauce.

SERVES 6
HANDS-ON 28 min.
TOTAL 28 min.

1 lb. ground sirloin
1 lb. ground chuck
1 tsp. table salt
½ tsp. freshly ground black pepper
⅓ cup pickled sliced jalapeño peppers, minced
6 (¼-inch-thick) pineapple slices
6 hamburger buns
 Cilantro-Jalapeño Cream
 Toppings: avocado slices, fresh cilantro sprigs, diced red onion

1. Light charcoal grill or preheat gas grill to 350° to 400° (**medium-high**). Gently combine first 4 ingredients. Stir in minced jalapeño peppers, and shape into 6 (5-inch) patties.

2. Grill patties, covered with grill lid, 4 to 5 minutes on each side or until center is no longer pink. Grill pineapple 1 to 2 minutes on each side. Serve burgers on buns; top burgers with Cilantro-Jalapeño Cream, grilled pineapple slices, avocado slices, cilantro sprigs, and diced onion.

CILANTRO-JALAPEÑO CREAM

Makes: ¾ cup   Hands-on: 10 min.   Total: 40 min.

½ cup sour cream
¼ cup chopped fresh cilantro
1 medium jalapeño pepper, seeded and minced
2 Tbsp. fresh lime juice

1. Combine all ingredients, and let stand at room temperature 30 minutes. To make ahead, refrigerate mixture in an airtight container up to 2 days.

STEP-BY-STEP

1. To ensure the burgers and pineapple come off at the same time, place the pineapple on the grill right after you flip the burgers.

GORGONZOLA-STUFFED HAMBURGERS

SERVES 4

HANDS-ON 22 min.

TOTAL 52 min.

Chilling the stuffed patties before grilling not only provides a great make-ahead bonus, but it also firms the cheese and patties so the stuffing stays inside and not on the grill.

1   (8-oz.) package sliced fresh mushrooms
2   Tbsp. butter, melted
¾   tsp. table salt, divided
1½ tsp. coarsely ground black pepper, divided
2   oz. cream cheese, softened
2   Tbsp. crumbled Gorgonzola cheese
1   Tbsp. grated onion
1   Tbsp. Dijon mustard
1½ lb. ground round
4   hamburger buns

1. Light charcoal grill or preheat gas grill to 350° to 400° (**medium-high**). Place mushrooms in a single layer in center of an 18- x 12-inch sheet of heavy-duty aluminum foil. Drizzle with butter; sprinkle with ¼ tsp. salt and ½ tsp. pepper. Bring up sides of foil over mushrooms; double fold top and side edges to seal, making a packet.

2. Stir together cream cheese and next 3 ingredients in a small bowl. Combine ground round, remaining 1 tsp. pepper, and remaining ½ tsp. salt in a large bowl just until blended (do not overwork mixture). Shape into 8 (4-inch) patties; spoon cheese mixture evenly into center of each of 4 patties. Top with remaining 4 patties, pressing edges to seal. Cover and chill 30 minutes.

3. Grill patties, covered with grill lid, 6 to 7 minutes on each side or until desired degree of doneness. At the same time, grill mushrooms, in foil packet, covered with grill lid, 10 minutes or until tender, turning once. Serve burgers on buns; top burgers evenly with mushroom mixture.

BBQ BACON BURGERS

Grill Vidalia onion slices alongside the burgers for an extra topping. Lettuce, tomato, and pickles also pair well with these saucy burgers.

1½ lb. ground round

1¼ tsp. table salt

¼ tsp. freshly ground black pepper

½ cup barbecue sauce, divided

4 slices white Cheddar cheese

4 sesame seed hamburger buns

8 cooked bacon slices

1. Light charcoal grill or preheat gas grill to 350° to 400° (**medium-high**). Shape ground round into 4 (4-inch) patties. Sprinkle with salt and pepper.

2. Place patties on cooking grate, and brush with 2 Tbsp. barbecue sauce. Grill patties, covered with grill lid, 5 minutes; turn patties over, and brush with 2 Tbsp. barbecue sauce. Grill 5 minutes or until center is no longer pink. Top each burger with 1 slice cheese; grill, covered with grill lid, 1 minute or until cheese melts.

3. Serve burgers on buns; top burgers with bacon and remaining barbecue sauce.

David's TIPS

The internal temperature of a cooked burger needs to reach 160° to be safe to eat. The days of the medium-rare burger are a thing of the past. Use safety first, but you don't have to compromise flavor. The best way to get a reading on your burger is with a digital thermometer. They easily take the temperature of burgers and small pieces of meat, because the sensors are on the bottom half inch of the stems.

THE BEEFY BURGER

When my buddy, chef Linton Hopkins, began developing his famous Holeman and Finch burger, he got me thinking about the humble meat patty's origins. This particular recipe is about honoring the hamburger in its simplicity. It boils down to highlighting the beef—a carefully selected blend of equal parts sirloin and brisket—with one slice of American cheese, a sweet splash of ketchup, some bright, acidic mustard, and pickles and onions. What you end up with is simple perfection.

SERVES 8
HANDS-ON 15 min.
TOTAL 15 min.

1   lb. ground sirloin
1   lb. ground brisket
    Kosher salt
    Freshly ground black pepper
8   potato rolls
½   cup unsalted butter, melted
    Toppings: thinly sliced Vidalia onions, bread-and-butter or dill pickle slices, ketchup, yellow mustard

1. Light charcoal grill or preheat gas grill to 350° to 400° (**medium-high**). Combine sirloin and brisket, and shape into 8 (4-oz.) patties. Sprinkle burgers with salt and pepper, and place on cooking grate; grill until medium or until a meat thermometer inserted into thickest portion registers 160° (about 10 minutes).

2. Brush inside of top and bottom of each roll with melted butter, and grill 45 seconds to 1 minute or until well toasted. Serve burgers on toasted rolls with desired toppings.

PRIME CHOICE

I've learned the importance in life of befriending the four Bs: your barista, your bartender, your barber, and your butcher—especially the latter. Treat your butcher right, and he or she can do wonders for you. You'll get the best cuts of meat whenever you need them.

SLOPPY JOE CAROLINA-STYLE BURGERS

SERVES 4

HANDS-ON 20 min.

TOTAL 30 min.

⅓ cup mayonnaise

⅓ cup sour cream

1 Tbsp. apple cider vinegar

1½ tsp. kosher salt, divided

¾ tsp. freshly ground black pepper, divided

1 (16-oz.) package 3-color deli coleslaw mix

1 lb. ground sirloin

2 Tbsp. steak sauce

4 hamburger buns, toasted

1 (16-oz.) can chili, warmed

1. Light charcoal grill or preheat gas grill to 350° to 400° (**medium-high**). Whisk together mayonnaise, sour cream, vinegar, ½ tsp. salt, and ¼ tsp. pepper in a large bowl. Add coleslaw mix; toss to coat. Cover and chill until ready to serve.

2. Gently combine ground sirloin, steak sauce, and remaining 1 tsp. salt and remaining ½ tsp. pepper. Shape into 4 (4-inch) patties. Grill patties, covered with grill lid, 4 to 5 minutes on each side or until no longer pink in center. Serve burgers on toasted buns; top burgers with chili and coleslaw mixture.

PIGGY BURGERS

SERVES 4

HANDS-ON 20 min.

TOTAL 20 min.

This is one burger you want to cook well done. Be sure to take the temperature of your patties before serving; it should register 145°F.

1 lb. ground pork

4 thick bacon slices, cooked and crumbled

2 tsp. molasses-bacon seasoning blend

4 hamburger buns, toasted

Toppings: onion-flavored pickles, bottled barbecue sauce

1. Light charcoal grill or preheat gas grill to 350° to 400° (**medium-high**). Gently combine first 3 ingredients; shape into 4 (4-inch) patties.

2. Grill patties, covered with grill lid, 5 minutes on each side or until no longer pink in center. Serve burgers on buns with desired toppings.

PRIME CHOICE

If you don't see ground pork in the supermarket, ask the butcher to grind it for you. Choose a blend that's not too fatty, such as an 85/15 mix of lean to fat.

Sloppy Joe Carolina-Style Burger

Piggy Burger

Pimiento Cheese–
Bacon Burgers

PIMIENTO CHEESE–BACON BURGERS

Let the patties stand at room temperature for 10 minutes before grilling.

1 lb. ground sirloin
1 lb. ground chuck
1 tsp. table salt
½ tsp. freshly ground black pepper
¼ cup mixed chopped fresh

herbs (such as basil, mint, and oregano)
6 hamburger buns, toasted
Toppings: pimiento cheese, cooked bacon slices, lettuce, and tomato slices

SERVES 6
HANDS-ON 28 min.
TOTAL 38 min.

1. Light charcoal grill or preheat gas grill to 350° to 400° (**medium-high**). Combine first 4 ingredients gently; stir in herbs. Shape mixture into 6 (5-inch) patties; let stand 10 minutes.

2. Grill, covered with grill lid, 4 to 5 minutes on each side or until beef is no longer pink in center. Serve burgers on toasted buns. Top each burger with cheese, bacon, lettuce, and tomato.

SUN-DRIED TOMATO–PESTO BURGERS

For more Mediterranean flavor, add chopped Kalamata olives to the meat mixture, but take the salt down by half.

1 lb. ground sirloin
1 lb. ground chuck
1 tsp. table salt
½ tsp. freshly ground black pepper
1 (3-oz.) package sun-dried

tomato halves, chopped
1 garlic clove, pressed
6 hamburger buns, toasted
Toppings: refrigerated pesto, sliced goat cheese, and sliced pepperoncini salad peppers

SERVES 6
HANDS-ON 28 min.
TOTAL 38 min.

1. Light charcoal grill or preheat gas grill to 350° to 400° (**medium-high**). Combine first 4 ingredients gently; stir in chopped sun-dried tomatoes and garlic. Shape mixture into 6 (5-inch) patties; let stand 10 minutes.

2. Grill, covered with grill lid, 4 to 5 minutes on each side or until beef is no longer pink in center. Serve burgers on toasted buns. Top each burger with pesto, cheese, and peppers.

GRILLED CHICKEN TEQUILA BURGERS

SERVES 5

HANDS-ON 20 min.

TOTAL 40 min.

Tequila and soy sauce add flavor and act as a tenderizer. Be sure not to overcook the patties, as ground chicken can dry out quickly.

1 lb. ground chicken breast

3 Tbsp. chopped fresh cilantro

2 garlic cloves, chopped

1 jalapeño pepper, seeded and chopped

½ cup panko (Japanese bread-crumbs) or ¼ cup uncooked regular or quick-cooking oats

2 Tbsp. tequila

1 tsp. lime zest

¾ tsp. table salt

½ tsp. freshly ground black pepper

¼ tsp. soy sauce

Sliced bell peppers

Sliced onions

5 hamburger buns

Cilantro-Lime Mayonnaise

1. Light charcoal grill or preheat gas grill to 350° to 400° (**medium-high**). Pulse ground chicken, cilantro, garlic, and jalapeño pepper in a food processor 3 to 4 times or until combined. Add panko or oats, tequila, lime zest, salt, pepper, and soy sauce; pulse until combined. Shape into 5 patties.

2. Grill patties, covered with grill lid, 4 to 5 minutes on each side or until a meat thermometer inserted in thickest portion registers 165°; remove from grill, and keep warm. Grill sliced bell peppers and onions 4 minutes on each side or until tender. Serve burgers on buns; top burgers with Cilantro-Lime Mayonnaise and grilled bell pepper and onion slices.

CILANTRO-LIME MAYONNAISE

Makes: ¾ cup   Hands-on: 5 min.   Total: 5 min.

¾ cup mayonnaise

1 tsp. chopped fresh cilantro

1 tsp. chopped fresh chives

1 tsp. lime zest

1 tsp. fresh lime juice

1. Stir together all ingredients.

GRILLED SMOKED BOLOGNA WITH YELLOW MUSTARD SLAW

I grew up just a few blocks from the Bunny Bread factory in New Orleans. The irresistible smells of freshly baked bread filled the neighborhood, taunting me because white bread was strictly forbidden in my house. My bologna sandwiches—which I frequently traded at school lunch— were stacked on slices of fiber-rich whole wheat. Now, I get to make my own rules, and sometimes I just want grilled bologna on extra-thick white bread.

> **SERVES 8**
> **HANDS-ON 24 min.**
> **TOTAL 54 min.**

1 head green cabbage, quartered	½ tsp. celery seeds
3 Tbsp. extra virgin olive oil	¼ tsp. ground red pepper
Table salt	½ cup grated Vidalia onion
Freshly ground black pepper	8 (½-inch-thick) slices bologna
¼ cup mayonnaise	Wood chips
3 Tbsp. yellow mustard	16 slices Texas toast
	¾ cup unsalted butter, melted

1. Light 1 side of charcoal grill or preheat gas grill to 350° to 400° (**medium-high**); leave other side unlit. Drizzle cabbage with oil, and season with salt and pepper. Place cabbage, cut sides down, on cooking grate; grill, turning occasionally, 7 minutes or until grill marks appear on all cut edges. Using a serrated knife, thinly slice the cabbage.

2. Combine mayonnaise, mustard, celery seeds, and red pepper in a large bowl, and mix until smooth. Add onion, and blend well; add sliced cabbage, and blend until thoroughly coated with dressing. Season with salt and freshly ground black pepper; refrigerate until ready to use.

3. Place bologna slices on cooking grate on lit side of grill, and grill 2 to 3 minutes on each side or until grill marks appear. Sprinkle wood chips over lit charcoal. Move bologna slices to unlit side of grill; cover with grill lid, and smoke for 10 minutes.

4. Brush 1 side of each slice of bread with melted butter, and place on cooking grate on lit side of grill; grill 45 seconds to 1 minute or until grill marks appear. Remove from grill (do not toast other side). Place 1 bologna slice on untoasted side of each of 8 bread slices; top each with ½ cup slaw and another bread slice, toasted side up.

David's TIPS

Prep the slaw dressing first, then throw the cabbage on the grill at the same time as the bologna. When the cabbage has a nice char, immediately transfer it to a cutting board to chop it up and dress it. Warm slaw adds great character to this sandwich.

SHRIMP BURGERS WITH SWEET 'N' SPICY TARTAR SAUCE

For an extra tang of flavor, grill lemon halves alongside the shrimp burgers. Squeeze a generous amount on each burger before topping it with tartar sauce.

SERVES 4
HANDS-ON 37 min.
TOTAL 1 hr., 37 min.

1¼ lb. unpeeled, medium-size raw shrimp

Vegetable cooking spray

1 large egg, lightly beaten

1 Tbsp. mayonnaise

2 tsp. lemon juice

½ tsp. table salt

⅛ tsp. ground red pepper

3 Tbsp. finely chopped celery

2 Tbsp. chopped green onion

1 Tbsp. chopped fresh parsley

1¼ cups crushed cornbread crackers (about 1 sleeve or 24 crackers)

4 Kaiser rolls with poppy seeds, split

Sweet 'n' Spicy Tartar Sauce

4 Bibb lettuce leaves

1. Peel shrimp; devein, if desired. Cut each shrimp into thirds.

2. Line a 15- x 10-inch jelly-roll pan with aluminum foil. Coat with cooking spray.

3. Stir together egg and next 4 ingredients; stir in celery, green onion, and parsley. Fold in shrimp and cracker crumbs (mixture will be thick). Shape into 4 (4-inch-wide, 1-inch-thick) patties; place on prepared pan. Cover and chill 1 to 24 hours. Transfer to freezer; freeze 30 minutes.

4. Coat cold cooking grate of grill with cooking spray, and place on grill. Light charcoal grill or preheat gas grill to 350° to 400° (**medium-high**). Grill burgers, covered with grill lid, 4 to 5 minutes or until burgers lift easily from cooking grate using a large spatula. Turn burgers, and grill 4 to 5 minutes or until shrimp turn pink and burgers are cooked through and lightly crisp. Grill buns, cut sides down, 1 to 2 minutes or until lightly toasted. Serve burgers on buns with Sweet 'n' Spicy Tartar Sauce and lettuce.

SWEET 'N' SPICY TARTAR SAUCE

Makes: 1 cup   Hands-on: 5 min.   Total: 35 min.

1 cup mayonnaise

2 Tbsp. chopped fresh parsley

2 Tbsp. horseradish

1½ tsp. Cajun seasoning

1½ tsp. lemon juice

¼ tsp. paprika

1. Stir together all ingredients. Cover and chill 30 minutes to 24 hours.

TEX-MEX TURKEY BURGERS

SERVES 6
HANDS-ON 25 min.
TOTAL 25 min.

This fork-and-knife burger pairs perfectly with a big batch of margaritas.

1   large lime
¼   cup finely chopped red onion
2   garlic cloves, minced
1   Tbsp. olive oil
1   cup fresh corn kernels (about 2 ears)
1   avocado, peeled and finely chopped
¼   cup finely chopped fresh cilantro leaves
1½ tsp. kosher salt, divided
1   lb. ground turkey
1   (4-oz.) can chopped green chiles
1   large egg, lightly beaten
½   tsp. ground cumin
½   cup fine, dry breadcrumbs
6   tostada shells, warmed
    Toppings: salsa verde, crumbled queso fresco
    Garnish: lime wedges

1. Light charcoal grill or preheat gas grill to 350° to 400° (**medium-high**). Grate zest from lime to equal 1 tsp. Cut lime in half, and squeeze juice from lime to equal 1 Tbsp.

2. Sauté onion and garlic in hot oil in a medium skillet 1 minute. Add corn, and cook 2 to 3 minutes or just until corn begins to brown. Transfer mixture to a medium bowl. Stir in lime zest, lime juice, avocado, cilantro, and ½ tsp. salt.

3. Combine turkey, next 4 ingredients, and remaining 1 tsp. salt. Gently shape mixture into 6 (4-inch) patties.

4. Grill patties, covered with grill lid, 4 to 5 minutes on each side or until done. Serve on tostada shells with corn mixture and desired toppings.

HERBED TURKEY BURGERS

Experiment with different herbs or even a blend such as rosemary and thyme for new, fresh flavor.

SERVES 4
HANDS-ON 10 min.
TOTAL 10 min.

1   lb. lean ground turkey
¼   cup chopped fresh basil
2   tsp. grated lemon rind
¾   tsp. minced garlic
⅛   tsp. table salt
4   kaiser rolls, split
    Toppings: shredded spinach leaves, tomato slices

1. Light charcoal grill or preheat gas grill to 350° to 400° (**medium-high**). Combine first 5 ingredients in a large bowl just until blended (do not overwork mixture). Shape into 4 (5-inch) patties.

2. Grill patties, covered with grill lid, 5 to 6 minutes on each side or until desired degree of doneness.

3. Scoop out soft centers of bottom half of rolls, leaving ¼-inch-thick shells. Place burgers in shells; top evenly with spinach and tomato slices, and cover with roll tops.

David's TIPS

Keep your thermometer clean! Do NOT stick a thermometer back into the burger without cleaning it first. You are just dragging uncooked juices back in and that can be dangerous if cooking with burgers using poultry meats.

FEATHERED FEZ TURKEY BURGERS

SERVES 4
HANDS-ON 13 min.
TOTAL 13 min.

My wife doesn't eat beef or pork, so we make a lot of turkey burgers at our house. It's an art we've come to perfect over the years. Traditionally, turkey burgers tend to be dry because there's very little fat content, so we pile our burgers high with veggies that hold moisture and slather on a boldly flavored olive spread.

1   lb. ground turkey (thigh meat)
3   Tbsp. Worcestershire sauce
1   tsp. kosher salt
4   potato rolls
½   cup unsalted butter, melted
⅓   cup spicy green olive tapenade
½   cup mayonnaise
    Toppings: grilled portobello mushrooms, feta or goat cheese, grilled sweet onions, fresh baby spinach, sliced fresh tomatoes

1. Light charcoal grill or preheat gas grill to 350° to 400° (**medium-high**). Combine turkey and Worcestershire sauce, and shape into 4 (4-oz.) patties. Sprinkle burgers with salt, and place on cooking grate; grill 3 to 3½ minutes on each side or until a meat thermometer inserted into thickest portion registers 165°.

2. Brush inside of top and bottom of each roll with melted butter, and grill 45 seconds to 1 minute or until well toasted. Meanwhile, combine tapenade and mayonnaise, and mix well. Serve burgers on toasted buns with tapenade mixture and desired toppings.

David's TIPS

To test for doneness, make a slit on 1 side of a browned burger. If juice is cloudy and brown, cook 30 seconds to 1 minute more.

LAMB BURGERS

1   cup fat-free Greek yogurt
½   cup grated cucumber
1   tsp. finely chopped fresh mint
3   garlic cloves, pressed and divided
1¾ tsp. table salt, divided
2   lb. ground lamb

¼   cup minced red onion
¼   cup chopped fresh mint
1   Tbsp. chopped fresh oregano
1   Tbsp. whole grain mustard
6   hamburger buns
     Toppings: Bibb lettuce leaves, sliced tomatoes, sliced red onion, dill pickle chips

1. Light charcoal grill or preheat gas grill to 350° to 400° (**medium-high**). Stir together first 3 ingredients, 1 pressed garlic clove, and ½ tsp. salt. Cover and chill.

2. Gently combine lamb, next 4 ingredients, remaining 2 garlic cloves, and remaining 1¼ tsp. salt. Shape into 6 (4-inch) patties.

3. Grill patties, covered with grill lid, 5 to 6 minutes on each side or until desired degree of doneness. Serve on buns with sauce and desired toppings.

PLUM-GLAZED SAUSAGES

¾   cup plum preserves
2   Tbsp. balsamic vinegar
2   tsp. chopped fresh thyme

¼   tsp. freshly ground black pepper
2   lb. assorted fresh sausages

1. Light charcoal grill or preheat gas grill to 300° to 350° (**medium**). Cook first 4 ingredients in a small saucepan over low heat, stirring often, 5 minutes; reserve half of mixture.

2. Grill sausages, covered with grill lid, 10 to 12 minutes or until desired degree of doneness, turning occasionally and brushing with remaining half of plum mixture during last 5 minutes of grilling. Remove from heat; let stand 5 minutes. Serve with reserved plum mixture.

Plum-Glazed
Sausages

GRILLED ANDOUILLE SAUSAGE

Traditional Cajun andouille sausages are made from pork, usually Boston butt, heavily smoked and spicy. The distinctive aroma inspires tastes of earthy deliciousness and the ultimate complement of sweet bread 'n' butter pickles.

SERVES 8
HANDS-ON 12 min.
TOTAL 5 hr., 32 min.

2 lb. andouille sausage
   Bread-and-Butter Pickles

1. Light charcoal grill or preheat gas grill to 350° to 400° (**medium-high**). Grill sausage, turning occasionally, 5 minutes or until desired degree of doneness.

2. Cut sausage diagonally into ¼-inch-thick slices, and serve with Bread-and-Butter Pickles.

BREAD-AND-BUTTER PICKLES

Makes: 14 (1-pt.) jars   Hands-on: 2 hr., 10 min.   Total: 5 hr., 20 min.

25 to 35 medium cucumbers (about 9½ lb.)	4 cups sugar
8 large onions	2 Tbsp. mustard seeds
2 large bell peppers	1 tsp. ground turmeric
½ cup pickling salt	½ tsp. whole cloves
5 cups white vinegar	14 (1-pt.) hot, sterilized canning jars, lids, and bands

1. Cut cucumbers into ¼-inch-thick slices and onions into ⅛-inch-thick slices. Chop bell peppers. Place vegetables in a bowl; toss with pickling salt. Let stand 3 hours; drain.

2. Bring vinegar and next 4 ingredients to a boil in a large stockpot; boil just until sugar dissolves. Add drained cucumber mixture, and cook, stirring often, 7 to 10 minutes or until mixture is thoroughly heated and cucumber peels turn dark green.

3. Pack half of hot mixture into 7 (1-pt.) hot, sterilized canning jars, filling to ½ inch from top; remove air bubbles by gently stirring with a long wooden skewer. Cover at once with metal lids, and screw on bands; process in boiling water bath 10 minutes. Repeat procedure with remaining mixture and remaining 7 hot, sterilized jars, lids, and bands.

SWEET HEAT HOT DOGS

SERVES 8
HANDS-ON 30 min.
TOTAL 30 min.

Surprise your guests with this less traditional hot dog sandwich topped with chopped sweet-hot pickles, crunchy shredded red cabbage, and homemade Sriracha mayonnaise.

¾ cup mayonnaise

1 Tbsp. whole grain mustard

1 green onion, minced

2 Tbsp. Asian hot chili sauce (such as Sriracha)

8 hot dogs

8 hot dog buns, toasted

1 cup chopped sweet-hot pickles

2 cups shredded red cabbage

1. Light charcoal grill or preheat gas grill to 350° to 400° (**medium-high**). Combine first 3 ingredients and 1 Tbsp. chili sauce in a small bowl. Brush hot dogs with remaining 1 Tbsp. chili sauce.

2. Grill hot dogs, covered with grill lid, 4 to 6 minutes or until thoroughly heated. Serve hot dogs in toasted buns. Top with mayonnaise mixture, and sprinkle with chopped pickles and shredded cabbage.

GRILLED SAUSAGE WITH ASPARAGUS

SERVES 4 to 6
HANDS-ON 20 min.
TOTAL 35 min.

3 lemons, halved and divided

½ cup refrigerated pesto sauce

½ cup toasted walnuts, chopped and divided

2 lb. fresh asparagus

2 Tbsp. olive oil

2 lb. sweet Italian sausage links

1. Light charcoal grill or preheat gas grill to 350° to 400° (**medium-high**). Squeeze juice from 2 lemon halves to equal 2 Tbsp. Stir together lemon juice, pesto, and ¼ cup walnuts. Snap off and discard tough ends of asparagus; toss asparagus with oil.

2. Grill sausage, without grill lid, 10 minutes or until thoroughly cooked, turning occasionally. At the same time, grill asparagus, without grill lid, 4 minutes or until tender. Brush asparagus with pesto mixture, and transfer to a serving platter. Grill remaining 4 lemon halves, cut sides down, 1 minute or until charred; place on platter with asparagus. Slice sausage, and add to platter. Sprinkle with remaining ¼ cup walnuts.

Sweet Heat
Hot Dogs

BIRDS

ON FRIDAY AND SATURDAY AFTERNOONS on the wide-wood-planked deck of my parents' backyard, you could find my father armed with a basting brush in one hand and a cold one and cigar in the other. The air is streaked with the varied scents of a musky cloud of his Cuban-style cigar and the currents of hardwood smoke coming from the sizzling chicken on his PK Portable Kitchen Grill. I was about 7 years old and eye-level to the grill the first time I witnessed the magic at work and smelled its rewards. To dad, it was his basic chicken, but to us it was extraordinary. With every bite you got the nose-tickling aroma of his sauce, a savory scent both tangy and deliciously rich.

The key to an excellent grilled chicken is just as much the sauce as the heat source. Wood chips are essential for flavor—oak, cherry, or hickory—and must burn way down on the coals before you put anything on the grates. You do not want the chicken to take on too much essence of the coal. Once your grill is prepped, then place the thighs, wings, and breasts right on the heat, alternating basting and rearranging the birds on the grill. My father's theory is when the juices are dripping down onto the coals, the bird is thirsty, so keep giving it moisture. I've always followed this advice and it has never failed. Father does know best.

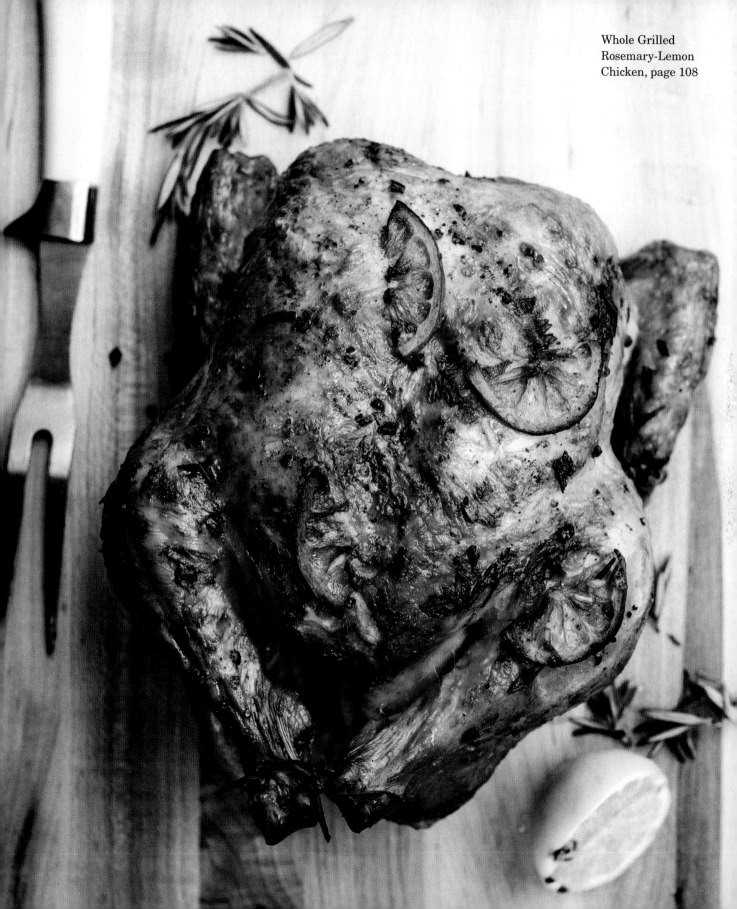

Whole Grilled
Rosemary-Lemon
Chicken, page 108

MARINATED CHICKEN QUARTERS

SERVES 4

HANDS-ON 1 hr.

TOTAL 1 hr., plus
8 hr. for marinating

You can use bone-in chicken breasts in place of the chicken quarters.

½ cup butter, melted

½ cup fresh lemon juice

1 Tbsp. paprika

1 Tbsp. dried oregano

1 tsp. garlic salt

1 Tbsp. chopped fresh cilantro

1 tsp. ground cumin

1 (2½-lb.) whole chicken, quartered

½ tsp. table salt

½ tsp. freshly ground black pepper

1. Whisk together first 7 ingredients; reserve ½ cup butter mixture for basting, and chill.

2. Sprinkle chicken evenly with salt and pepper. Place in a shallow dish or zip-top plastic freezer bag; pour remaining butter mixture over chicken. Cover or seal, and chill 8 hours.

3. Light charcoal grill or preheat gas grill to 350° to 400° (**medium-high**). Remove chicken from marinade; discard marinade. Grill chicken, covered with grill lid, 40 to 45 minutes or until a meat thermometer inserted into thickest portion registers 165°, basting often with reserved butter mixture and turning once.

GRILLED CHICKEN AND NEW POTATOES

SERVES 4
HANDS-ON 20 min.
TOTAL 20 min.

For fuss-free cooking, seal the leeks and potatoes (or any other vegetables) in a foil packet before placing them on the grill.

1   medium leek
1½ lb. small new potatoes, halved
2   Tbsp. crushed red pepper-and-garlic seasoning (such as McCormick), divided
4   Tbsp. olive oil, divided
1½ tsp. table salt, divided
1½ lb. chicken breast tenders
2   Tbsp. fresh lemon juice, divided
2   bunches green onions

1. Light charcoal grill or preheat gas grill to 350° to 400° (**medium-high**). Remove and discard root end and dark green top of leek. Cut in half lengthwise, and rinse thoroughly under cold running water to remove grit and sand. Cut into thin slices.

2. Toss together leek, potatoes, 1 Tbsp. garlic seasoning, 3 Tbsp. oil, and 1 tsp. salt. Place half of the leek mixture in the center of each of 2 large pieces of heavy-duty aluminum foil. Bring up sides of foil over leek mixture; double fold top and sides to seal, making packets. Grill leek mixture, in foil packets, covered with grill lid, 12 minutes.

3. Meanwhile, toss together chicken, 1 Tbsp. lemon juice, remaining 1 Tbsp. garlic seasoning, remaining 1 Tbsp. oil, and remaining ½ tsp. salt.

4. Shake foil packets, using tongs, and return to grill. At the same time, grill chicken, covered with grill lid, 5 minutes; turn chicken. Place green onions on grill, and grill chicken, green onions, and foil packets 4 to 5 minutes or until a meat thermometer inserted into thickest portion of chicken registers 165°.

PRIME CHOICE

Leeks are naturally mellower than their other allium counterparts. If you can't find leeks in your local grocer, sliced yellow onions may be substituted.

GRILLED CHICKEN WITH FRESH CORNCAKES

3   lemons

2   garlic cloves, pressed

⅓   cup olive oil

1   tsp. Dijon mustard

¼   tsp. freshly ground black pepper

1½ tsp. table salt, divided

3   skinned and boned chicken breasts

3   ears fresh corn, husks removed

1   Tbsp. olive oil

1   (6-oz.) package buttermilk cornbread mix

¼   cup chopped fresh basil

8   thick hickory-smoked bacon slices, cooked

2   cups loosely packed arugula

SERVES 4
HANDS-ON 15 min.
TOTAL 56 min.

1. Light charcoal grill or preheat gas grill to 350° to 400° (**medium-high**). Grate zest from lemons to equal 1 Tbsp. Cut lemons in half; squeeze juice from lemons into a measuring cup to equal ¼ cup.

2. Whisk together lemon zest, lemon juice, garlic, next 3 ingredients, and 1 tsp. salt; reserve ¼ cup lemon mixture. Pour remaining lemon mixture into a large zip-top plastic freezer bag; add chicken. Seal and chill 15 minutes, turning once. Remove chicken from marinade; discard marinade.

3. Brush corn with 1 Tbsp. oil; sprinkle with remaining ½ tsp. salt.

4. Grill chicken and corn at the same time, covered with grill lid, 20 minutes or until a meat thermometer inserted into thickest portion of chicken registers 165°. Turn chicken once and corn every 4 to 5 minutes. Remove chicken, and cover with aluminum foil. Hold each grilled cob upright on a cutting board, and carefully cut downward, cutting kernels from cob.

5. Stir together cornbread mix and ⅔ cup water in a small bowl until smooth. Stir in basil and 1 cup grilled corn kernels. Pour about ¼ cup batter for each corncake onto a hot, lightly greased griddle. Cook corncakes 3 to 4 minutes or until tops are covered with bubbles and edges look dry and cooked; turn and cook other side.

6. Thinly slice chicken. To serve, place 2 corncakes on each plate, top with chicken and 2 bacon slices. Toss arugula with reserved ¼ cup lemon mixture. Place arugula on bacon, and sprinkle with remaining grilled corn kernels.

SWEET TEA—BRINED CHICKEN

SERVES 6 to 8

HANDS-ON 30 min.

TOTAL 2 hr., 35 min., plus 1 day for marinating

This sweet tea brine not only has enticingly juicy flavor, but the tannins in the tea act as a natural tenderizer, making the chicken extra moist.

2   family-size tea bags
½   cup firmly packed light brown sugar
¼   cup kosher salt
1   small sweet onion, thinly sliced
1   lemon, thinly sliced
3   garlic cloves, halved
2   (6-inch) fresh rosemary sprigs
1   Tbsp. freshly cracked black pepper
2   cups ice cubes
1   (3½- to 4-lb.) cut-up whole chicken

1. Bring 4 cups water to a boil in a 3-qt. heavy saucepan; add tea bags. Remove from heat; cover and steep 10 minutes.

2. Discard tea bags. Stir in sugar and next 6 ingredients, stirring until sugar dissolves. Cool completely (about 45 minutes); stir in ice. (Mixture should be cold before adding chicken.)

3. Place tea mixture and chicken in a large zip-top plastic freezer bag; seal. Place bag in a shallow baking dish, and chill 24 hours. Remove chicken from marinade; discard marinade. Pat chicken dry with paper towels.

4. Light 1 side of charcoal grill or preheat gas grill to 300° to 350° (**medium**); leave other side unlit. Place chicken pieces, skin sides down, over unlit side, and grill, covered with grill lid, 20 minutes. Turn chicken pieces, and grill, covered with grill lid, 40 to 50 minutes or until a meat thermometer inserted into thickest portion registers 165°. Transfer chicken, skin sides down, to lit side of grill, and grill 2 to 3 minutes or until skin is crisp. Let stand 5 minutes before serving.

David's
TIPS

For a more intense flavor, poke the chicken skin with a skewer to allow the sweet tea to penetrate.

CHIPOTLE-ORANGE CHICKEN LEGS

For a quick and cool side to accompany this sweet and spicy dish, combine 1 (16-oz.) package shredded coleslaw mix, 1 (8-oz.) container sour cream, 2 Tbsp. fresh lemon juice, and 1 tsp. table salt. Cover and chill until ready to serve.

SERVES 4 to 6
HANDS-ON 20 min.
TOTAL 50 min.

1   cup fresh orange juice, divided
5   Tbsp. soy sauce, divided
3   Tbsp. brown sugar
2   Tbsp. olive oil
6   garlic cloves, pressed
1   Tbsp. orange zest
1½ tsp. kosher salt
1   tsp. ground chipotle chile pepper
2   lb. chicken drumsticks (about 8 drumsticks)
2   tsp. brown sugar
2   tsp. cornstarch

1. Light charcoal grill or preheat gas grill to 350° to 400° (**medium-high**). Combine ¼ cup orange juice, 3 Tbsp. soy sauce, 3 Tbsp. brown sugar, and next 5 ingredients in a shallow dish or large zip-top plastic freezer bag; add chicken. Cover or seal, and chill 10 minutes. Remove chicken from marinade; discard marinade.

2. Grill chicken, covered with grill lid, 10 to 12 minutes on each side or until a meat thermometer inserted into thickest portion registers 165°. Remove from grill; cover with aluminum foil, and let stand 10 minutes.

3. Meanwhile, whisk together 2 tsp. brown sugar, remaining ¾ cup orange juice, and remaining 2 Tbsp. soy sauce in a small saucepan. Whisk together cornstarch and 2 tsp. water, and whisk into orange juice mixture. Bring mixture to a boil over medium heat, and cook, whisking constantly, 1 minute or until thickened. Brush sauce over chicken before serving.

BEER-CAN CHICKEN

SERVES 4
HANDS-ON 20 min.
TOTAL 2 hr., 35 min.

Light or dark beer makes no difference in the flavor of the chicken, so use whichever style of beer you prefer to drink while grilling.

1   (4-lb.) whole chicken
1   Tbsp. vegetable oil
1½ Tbsp. Smoky-Sweet BBQ Rub (page 25)

1½ tsp. kosher salt
1   (12-oz.) can beer

1. If applicable, remove neck and giblets from chicken, and reserve for another use. Pat chicken dry with paper towels. Brush cavity and outside of chicken with oil. Stir together Smoky-Sweet Barbecue Rub and salt; sprinkle mixture inside cavity and on outside of chicken. Chill chicken 30 minutes or up to 12 hours.

2. Light 1 side of charcoal grill or preheat gas grill to to 350° to 400° (**medium-high**); leave other side unlit. Open beer can; place chicken upright on can, fitting can into cavity. Pull legs forward to form a tripod so chicken stands upright.

3. Place chicken upright on unlit side of grill. Grill chicken, covered with grill lid, 1 to 1½ hours or until golden and a meat thermometer inserted in thickest portion registers 165°. Carefully remove chicken from can. Cover chicken loosely with aluminum foil; let stand 10 minutes before serving.

GRILLED SALT-AND-PEPPER CHICKEN WINGS

½ cup honey
¼ cup bottled chili sauce
2 Tbsp. fresh lemon juice
2 lb. chicken wings
2 Tbsp. olive oil
1½ tsp. kosher salt
½ teaspoon freshly ground black pepper

SERVES 6 to 8
HANDS-ON 10 min.
TOTAL 35 min.

1. Combine honey, chili sauce, and lemon juice in a small saucepan; place over medium heat, and cook, stirring often, 2 minutes or until thoroughly heated. Set aside.

2. Light charcoal grill or preheat gas grill to 350° to 400° (**medium-high**). Toss together wings and oil in a large bowl. Sprinkle with salt and pepper, and toss to coat. Grill wings, covered with grill lid, 25 to 30 minutes or until skin is crisp and a meat thermometer inserted into thickest portion registers 165°, turning occasionally. Drizzle with honey mixture before serving.

BRICK GRILLED CORNISH HENS

8 (1½- to 1¾-lb.) Cornish hens
3 Tbsp. kosher salt
3 Tbsp. freshly ground black pepper
3 Tbsp. minced garlic
3 Tbsp. chopped fresh rosemary
1 Tbsp. dried crushed red pepper
¼ cup fresh lemon juice
¼ cup olive oil
8 aluminum foil-wrapped bricks
Garnishes: lemon wedges, flat-leaf parsley sprigs

SERVES 8
HANDS-ON 15 min.
TOTAL 1 hr., 48 min.

1. Cut hens lengthwise through the backbone using kitchen shears; flatten. Combine salt and next 4 ingredients; rub over hens. Place in 2-qt. zip-top plastic freezer bags or 2 large baking dishes. Whisk together lemon juice and olive oil; drizzle over hens. Seal or cover; chill 1 to 24 hours. Remove hens from marinade, discarding marinade.

2. Light charcoal grill or preheat gas grill to 300° to 350° (**medium**). Place hens on cooking grate of grill; top each with a brick. Grill, covered with grill lid, 18 to 20 minutes on each side. Turn grill off, and let stand, covered with grill lid, 5 to 8 minutes or until a meat thermometer inserted into thickest portion registers 165°.

David's TIPS

Cast-iron skillets may be substituted for foil-wrapped bricks. Place foil between skillet and hen.

SMOKED CHICKEN WITH FRESH HERB MARINADE

SERVES 4

HANDS-ON 20 min.

TOTAL 2 hr., 20 min.,
plus 8 hr. for marinating

Cooking the chicken in a disposable pan, instead of directly on the grill grate, helps keep it moist, while the herb-lemon juice marinade enhances the natural flavors.

6   Tbsp. olive oil

¼   cup peanut oil

¼   cup chopped fresh flat-leaf parsley

2   Tbsp. chopped fresh basil

2   Tbsp. chopped fresh oregano

2   Tbsp. fresh lemon juice

2   Tbsp. Dijon mustard

4   tsp. dark brown sugar

4   tsp. Worcestershire

1   garlic clove, minced

2   tsp. table salt

½   tsp. freshly ground black pepper

1   (3- to 3½-lb.) whole chicken, halved

1   cup hickory chips

1. Whisk together first 12 ingredients. Pour mixture into a 1-gal. zip-top plastic freezer bag; add chicken. Seal bag, and turn to coat. Chill 8 to 12 hours.

2. Light 1 side of charcoal grill or preheat gas grill to 300° to 350° (**medium**); leave other side unlit.

3. Remove chicken from marinade, reserving marinade. Place chicken, skin-sides up, in a 13- x 9-inch disposable aluminum foil pan; pour marinade over chicken. Sprinkle hickory chips over hot coals. Place pan with chicken on unlit side of grill.

4. Grill chicken, covered with grill lid, 2 hours or until a meat thermometer inserted in thickest portion registers 165°. Spoon pan drippings over chicken before serving.

CHICKEN BREASTS WITH MUSHROOMS AND ASPARAGUS

Serve this Mediterranean-inspired dish with lightly dressed greens or chopped tomatoes.

SERVES 4
HANDS-ON 10 min.
TOTAL 20 min.

4   skinned and boned chicken breasts (about 1½ lb.)
2   tsp. Sicilian crushed red pepper-and-garlic seasoning
1   tsp. kosher salt
8   green onions (optional)
1   lb. fresh asparagus
1   (8-oz.) package sliced fresh mushrooms
3   garlic cloves, sliced
4   Tbsp. olive oil
2   Tbsp. drained capers
2   Tbsp. fresh lemon juice
¼   cup loosely packed fresh dill leaves or chopped fresh flat-leaf parsley
2   Tbsp. butter
4   French bread loaf slices, toasted

1. Light charcoal grill or preheat gas grill to 350° to 400° (**medium-high**). Place chicken between 2 sheets of heavy-duty plastic wrap; flatten to ¼-inch thickness, using a rolling pin or flat side of meat mallet. Sprinkle with seasoning and salt.

2. Grill chicken, covered with grill lid, 4 to 5 minutes. Add green onions to grill, if desired; grill chicken and onions 4 to 5 minutes or until a meat thermometer inserted into thickest portion of chicken registers 165°.

3. Snap off and discard tough ends of asparagus. Cook asparagus and next 2 ingredients in hot oil in a large nonstick skillet over medium-high heat, stirring often, 3 to 4 minutes or until asparagus is crisp-tender. Add capers and lemon juice; cook 1 to 2 minutes, stirring to loosen browned bits from bottom of skillet. Remove from heat; stir in dill or parsley and butter, stirring until butter melts. Place chicken and onions on bread slices, and top with sauce.

PRIME CHOICE

Sicilian spice adds a punch of flavor, but if you can't find it in your local grocer, season the chicken liberally with freshly ground black pepper and salt.

WHOLE GRILLED ROSEMARY-LEMON CHICKEN

SERVES 6

HANDS-ON 34 min.

TOTAL 2 hr., 29 min., plus 12 hr. for brining

Whole-animal grilling is a different ballgame from working with parts, but don't let the idea of it scare you away. This recipe stems from a classic whole roast chicken with herb butter smeared beneath the skin. On the grill it's important to avoid flare-ups from pockets of dripping fat, so instead of butter, I mash together a bright, acidic rosemary-lemon paste and massage it all over the chicken. If you choose to skip the brining step, be sure to add plenty of kosher salt to your paste.

½   cup kosher salt
1   (4- to 4½-lb.) chicken
½   lemon, sliced thin
2   Tbsp. fresh rosemary, chopped
2   Tbsp. minced garlic
3   Tbsp. olive oil
½   tsp. freshly ground black pepper
1   cup apple or pecan wood chips

1. Whisk together 6 cups water and salt in an 8-qt. container. Add chicken; cover and refrigerate at least 12 hours. About 1 hour before grilling the chicken, light charcoal grill or preheat gas grill to 250° to 300° (medium-low).

2. Combine lemon slices, rosemary, garlic, oil, and pepper in a mortar or other heavy bowl; use a pestle or back of a wooden spoon to slowly but firmly mash the ingredients together for 30 seconds. Remove chicken from brine; rinse under cold water, and pat dry with paper towels. Rub lemon mixture into skin; let stand 15 minutes.

3. Place chicken on cooking grate on lit side of grill. Grill 7 minutes or until grill marks and some charring appear; turn chicken over, and grill 7 more minutes. Move chicken to unlit side of grill, and sprinkle wood chips over hot coals. Grill, covered with grill lid, 1 to 1½ hours or until a meat thermometer inserted into thickest portion registers 165°. Remove chicken from grill, and let stand 10 minutes before serving.

David's TIPS

A meat thermometer is essential when cooking a whole bird. The best place to check the chicken's internal temperature is where the thigh meets the body of the bird. Insert the thermometer deep into the meat, close to the bone, and check for a temperature of 165°.

SWEET MUSTARD–GLAZED CHICKEN BREASTS

The tangy-sweet flavor combination of this marinade will work equally well with chicken or pork. Serve with hot cooked rice and steamed haricots verts to round out the meal.

<table>
<tr><td>SERVES 4</td></tr>
<tr><td>HANDS-ON 19 min.</td></tr>
<tr><td>TOTAL 49 min.</td></tr>
</table>

½   cup Dijon mustard
¼   cup maple syrup
2   Tbsp. white vinegar
2   Tbsp. lite soy sauce
½   tsp. coarsely ground black pepper
⅛   tsp. table salt
4   skinned and boned chicken breasts (about 2 lb.)

1. Light charcoal grill or preheat gas grill to 350° to 400° (**medium-high**). Whisk together first 6 ingredients in a small bowl. Reserve ½ cup mustard mixture to serve with cooked chicken.

2. Pour remaining ½ cup mustard mixture into a large shallow dish or zip-top plastic freezer bag; add chicken, turning to coat. Cover or seal, and chill 30 minutes. Remove chicken from marinade; discard marinade.

3. Grill chicken, covered with grill lid, 7 to 8 minutes on each side or until a meat thermometer inserted into thickest portion registers 165°. Serve with reserved ½ cup mustard mixture.

TOP-SHELF CHICKEN UNDER A "BRICK"

SERVES 4

HANDS-ON 45 min.

TOTAL 1 hr., 50 min.

In this recipe, "top-shelf" speaks to the crisp skin, superior flavor, and juiciness of the chicken. It also refers to cooking potatoes in the heavy cast-iron skillet that's used as a weight to press the chicken flat against the grill grate.

1 lb. small red or Yukon gold potatoes, halved

3 tsp. kosher salt, divided

1 (3- to 4-lb.) whole chicken

2 Tbsp. olive oil, divided

½ tsp. freshly ground black pepper

12 fresh herb sprigs (such as thyme, rosemary, sage, and tarragon)

2 lemons, halved

1. Bring potatoes, 1 tsp. salt, and water to cover to a boil in a large saucepan over high heat. Reduce heat to medium, and simmer 5 to 7 minutes or just until potatoes are tender; drain.

2. Light 1 side of charcoal grill or preheat gas grill to 300° to 350° (**medium**); leave other side unlit. Place chicken, breast side down, on a cutting board. Cut chicken, using kitchen shears, along both sides of backbone, separating backbone from chicken; discard backbone. Turn chicken, breast side up, and press firmly against breastbone with the heel of your hand until bone cracks. Tuck wing tips under, and rub with 1 Tbsp. oil. Sprinkle chicken with pepper and remaining 2 tsp. salt.

3. Heat a 12-inch cast-iron skillet on lit side of grill 10 minutes. Add remaining 1 Tbsp. oil to hot skillet; place potatoes, cut sides down, in skillet. Transfer skillet to unlit side of grill.

4. Place chicken, breast side down, over lit side of grill; top with herbs. Place cast-iron skillet with potatoes on foil-topped chicken to flatten. Grill, covered with grill lid, 10 to 15 minutes or until chicken is browned; remove skillet. Transfer chicken to unlit side of grill; place cast-iron skillet on chicken. Grill, covered with grill lid, 45 minutes or until a meat thermometer inserted in thickest portion of breast registers 165°. (For crisp skin, place chicken on lit side of grill, and grill, without grill lid, 5 additional minutes.) Remove skillet and chicken from grill, and let stand 5 minutes.

5. Meanwhile, place lemons, cut sides down, on lit side of grill, and grill, covered with grill lid, about 5 minutes or until charred and softened. Serve chicken with potatoes and charred lemon.

CHICKEN UNDER A SKILLET

SERVES 4

HANDS-ON 1 hr., 10 min.

TOTAL 2 hr., 15 min.

This recipe is inspired by a chicken dish I had in Italy that I remember vividly: The spatchcock bird was shallow-fried in a pan with another skillet on top. This version is done on the grill to add smoky flavor and a nice char.

1   (3- to 4-lb.) whole chicken

3   garlic cloves, peeled and quartered

1   cup loosely packed fresh flat-leaf parsley leaves

¼   cup extra virgin olive oil

1   Tbsp. fresh rosemary leaves

1   Tbsp. lemon zest

2   Tbsp. fresh lemon juice

1½ tsp. kosher salt

1½ tsp. herbes de Provence

1   tsp. freshly ground black pepper

1. Remove and discard giblets and neck from chicken; rinse chicken, and pat dry. Place chicken, breast side down, on a cutting board. Cut chicken, using kitchen shears, along both sides of backbone, separating backbone from chicken; discard backbone. Open chicken as you would a book. Turn chicken, breast side up, and press firmly against breastbone with the heel of your hand until bone cracks. Tuck wing tips under; place chicken in a baking dish or pan.

2. Pulse garlic and next 8 ingredients in a food processor until mixture forms a thick paste. Reserve half of paste; rub remaining paste on both sides of chicken. Cover with plastic wrap, and chill 1 hour.

3. Light 1 side of charcoal grill or preheat gas grill to 300° to 350° (medium); leave other side unlit. Place chicken, breast side down, over lit side of grill; top with a piece of aluminum foil. Place a cast-iron skillet on foil-topped chicken to flatten. Grill, covered with grill lid, 10 to 15 minutes or until chicken is browned; remove skillet and foil. Turn chicken over, and transfer to unlit side of grill. Grill, covered with grill lid, 45 minutes or until a meat thermometer inserted into thickest portion of breast registers 165°. Remove chicken from grill, and let stand 5 minutes. Brush with reserved paste before serving.

GRILLED CHIPOTLE CHICKEN THIGHS

Serve with sautéed tomatoes and okra to temper the heat in this fiery dish.

2   lb. skinned and boned chicken thighs
2   Tbsp. light brown sugar
½   tsp. dried oregano
½   tsp. ground chipotle chile pepper
½   tsp. kosher salt

SERVES 4
HANDS-ON 5 min.
TOTAL 12 min.

1. Light charcoal grill or preheat gas grill to 350° to 400° (**medium-high**). Place each chicken thigh between 2 sheets of heavy-duty plastic wrap, and flatten to ¼-inch thickness, using a rolling pin or flat side of a meat mallet. Combine sugar and next 3 ingredients; rub over chicken.

2. Grill chicken, covered with grill lid, 2 to 3 minutes on each side or until a meat thermometer inserted into thickest portion registers 165°. Remove from grill, and cover with aluminum foil to keep warm until ready to serve.

PRIME CHOICE

Chipotle chile peppers are smoke-dried jalapeños. They add a fiery heat to any dish.

SOUTH-OF-THE-BORDER BARBECUE CHICKEN

It's a Mexican fiesta in your mouth! This easy grilled chicken recipe is a crowd-pleaser you'll turn to again and again. Serve zesty Southwestern-flavored chicken over a bed of Mexican rice, or slice it to use in soft tacos.

SERVES 4
HANDS-ON 47 min.
TOTAL 47 min., plus 1 day for marinating

1½ cups fresh lime juice
1 cup olive oil
½ cup chopped fresh cilantro
2 tsp. seasoned salt
2 tsp. freshly ground black pepper
½ tsp. ancho chile powder
8 garlic cloves, minced
4 skinned and boned chicken breasts (about 2 lb.)

1. Whisk together first 7 ingredients in a small bowl; reserve 1 cup marinade for basting, and chill. Place remaining marinade in a large shallow dish or zip-top plastic freezer bag; add chicken, turning to coat. Cover or seal, and chill 24 hours, turning once.

2. Light charcoal grill or preheat gas grill to 300° to 350° (**medium**). Remove chicken from marinade; discard marinade. Grill chicken, covered with grill lid, 12 to 13 minutes on each side or until a meat thermometer inserted into thickest portion registers 165°, basting frequently with reserved 1 cup marinade.

SWEET GINGER CHICKEN THIGHS

SERVES 12

HANDS-ON 28 min.

TOTAL 38 min., plus 8 hr. for marinating

You can use either skin-on or skinless chicken thighs for this dish. Either way, monitor the grill carefully for flare-ups.

2   (6-oz.) cans pineapple juice
3   Tbsp. grated fresh ginger
3   Tbsp. soy sauce
2   Tbsp. sesame oil
2   Tbsp. light brown sugar
1   tsp. kosher salt
¾   tsp. coarsely ground black pepper
3   green onions, thinly sliced
4   lb. bone-in chicken thighs
Garnish: sliced green onions

1. Whisk together first 8 ingredients; reserve 1 cup for sauce. Pour remaining marinade into a large zip-top plastic freezer bag; add chicken. Seal and chill 8 hours.

2. Pour reserved 1 cup marinade into a small saucepan. Bring to a boil over medium-high heat; reduce heat, and simmer 10 minutes or until marinade is slightly thickened and reduced to ½ cup.

3. Light charcoal grill or preheat gas grill to 300° to 350° (**medium**). Remove chicken from marinade; discard marinade. Grill chicken, covered with grill lid, 8 to 10 minutes on each side or until a meat thermometer inserted into thickest portion registers 165°. Brush chicken with reserved marinade before serving.

LEMON-GARLIC DRUMSTICKS

SERVES 4 to 5

HANDS-ON 32 min.

TOTAL 32 min., plus 8 hr. for marinating

Look for the chicken marinade with white wine and herbs next to the Worcestershire sauce at your supermarket.

6   Tbsp. fresh lemon juice

¼   cup marinade for chicken with white wine and herbs

3   Tbsp. olive oil

1   tsp. kosher salt

1   tsp. freshly ground black pepper

8   garlic cloves, chopped

3   lb. chicken drumsticks

1. Combine lemon juice and next 5 ingredients in a large shallow dish or zip-top plastic freezer bag; add chicken, turning to coat. Cover or seal, and chill 8 to 24 hours, turning once.

2. Light charcoal grill or preheat gas grill to 300° to 350° (**medium**). Remove chicken from marinade; discard marinade. Grill chicken, covered with grill lid, 24 minutes or until a meat thermometer inserted into thickest portion registers 165°, turning often.

David's
TIPS

Be sure to discard the extra marinade. It isn't safe for consumption once it is used for the raw chicken.

SPICY GRILLED WINGS

These wings couldn't be easier to prepare, and the sauce is easily adjustable to fit your spice preference.

SERVES 12
HANDS-ON 1 hr.
TOTAL 1 hr.

2   tsp. ground chipotle chile pepper
2   tsp. freshly ground black pepper
2   tsp. table salt, divided
4½ to 5 lb. chicken wings
1   Tbsp. olive oil
3   Tbsp. butter
½   cup chopped onion
2   garlic cloves, pressed
1   cup cider vinegar
1   (8-oz.) can tomato sauce
1   (6-oz.) can tomato paste
2   Tbsp. light brown sugar
2   Tbsp. Worcestershire sauce
2   tsp. hot sauce
     Blue cheese dipping sauce

1. Light 1 side of charcoal grill or preheat gas grill to 350° to 400° (**medium-high**); leave other side unlit. Combine first 2 ingredients and 1 tsp. salt. Cut off chicken wing tips, and discard; cut wings in half at joint. Toss wings with oil; sprinkle with pepper mixture, and toss.

2. Arrange wings over unlit side of grill, and grill, covered with grill lid, 18 to 20 minutes on each side or until desired degree of doneness.

3. Meanwhile, melt butter in a saucepan over medium-high heat; add onion and garlic, and sauté 5 minutes or until tender. Reduce heat to medium; add vinegar, next 5 ingredients, and remaining 1 tsp. salt. Cook, stirring occasionally, 10 to 12 minutes or until bubbly.

4. Transfer wings to a clean bowl; add half of butter mixture, reserving remaining mixture. Toss wings gently to coat, and place on lit side of grill. Grill, covered with grill lid, 10 minutes or until browned and a meat thermometer inserted into thickest portion registers 165°, turning occasionally. Toss wings with reserved butter mixture. Serve with blue cheese dipping sauce.

CURRIED CHICKEN KABOBS

Moroccan seasoning blend contains cinnamon, cumin, turmeric, and pepper.

SERVES 4

HANDS-ON 23 min.

TOTAL 23 min.,
plus 1 day for marinating

- 4 skinned and boned chicken breasts, cut into 1½-inch pieces
- 1 Tbsp. Moroccan seasoning blend
- 1 tsp. kosher salt
- ¼ tsp. freshly ground black pepper
- ¾ cup fat-free yogurt
- 1 Tbsp. curry powder
- 2 Tbsp. fresh lime juice
- 1 Tbsp. grated fresh ginger
- 2 tsp. sugar
- ¼ tsp. ground red pepper
- 3 garlic cloves, minced
- Vegetable cooking spray
- 4 (12-inch) metal skewers
- 4 lime wedges

1. Toss chicken with Moroccan seasoning blend, ½ tsp. salt, and black pepper in a medium bowl. Stir together remaining ½ tsp. salt, yogurt, and next 6 ingredients in a small bowl. Pour ½ cup yogurt mixture into a large shallow dish or zip-top plastic freezer bag; add seasoned chicken, turning to coat. Cover or seal, and chill 24 hours. Cover and chill remaining ½ cup yogurt mixture to serve with cooked chicken.

2. Coat cold cooking grate with cooking spray, and place on grill. Light charcoal grill or preheat gas grill to 350° to 400° (**medium-high**).

3. Remove chicken from marinade; discard marinade. Thread chicken onto skewers, leaving ¼ inch space between pieces. Grill kabobs, covered with grill lid, 6 minutes on each side or until a meat thermometer inserted into thickest portion registers 165°. Serve kabobs with remaining chilled yogurt mixture and lime wedges.

STEP-BY-STEP

1. Leave ¼-inch space between chicken pieces to prevent the chicken from steaming.

2. Before lighting, spray the grill grates with cooking spray.

3. Place the skewers in an even line on the grill so it is easier to flip the chicken.

SMOKY CHICKEN BARBECUE KABOBS

SERVES 8
HANDS-ON 20 min.
TOTAL 20 min.

These kabobs feature a sprinkling of brown sugar mixed with smoked paprika and other spices, plus a tangy mayonnaise-based dipping sauce.

4   skinned and boned chicken breasts (about 2 lb.)
½   large red onion, cut into fourths and separated into pieces
1   pt. cherry tomatoes
8   (8-inch) metal skewers
     Smoky-Sweet BBQ Rub (page 25)
     White BBQ Sauce (page 30)

1. Light charcoal grill or preheat gas grill to 350° to 400° (**medium-high**). Cut chicken into 1-inch cubes. Thread chicken, onion pieces, and tomatoes alternately onto skewers, leaving ¼-inch space between pieces. Sprinkle kabobs with Smoky-Sweet Barbecue Rub.

2. Grill kabobs, covered with grill lid, 4 to 5 minutes on each side or until a meat thermometer inserted into thickest portion registers 165°. Serve with White Barbecue Sauce.

KOREAN BUTTERMILK CHICKEN KABOBS

Easily substitute pork or beef—both proteins work great with the sweet-spicy gochujang in the marinade—and you can play around with the fruit, too. Pineapple is a great stand-in for the lemon wedges.

1½ cups buttermilk

1 (10-oz.) bottle gochujang (Korean chili paste)

2 tsp. kosher salt

1 tsp. freshly ground black pepper

3 lb. skinned and boned chicken thighs, cut into 2-inch pieces

10 to 12 (10-inch) wooden or metal skewers

3 lemons

Vegetable cooking spray

½ cup torn fresh cilantro leaves

1. Stir together first 4 ingredients in a large shallow dish or zip-top plastic freezer bag. Add chicken, turning to coat. Cover or seal, and chill 1 to 3 hours.

2. Meanwhile, soak wooden skewers in water 30 minutes (omit if using metal skewers). Cut each lemon into 8 wedges.

3. Coat cold cooking grate with cooking spray, and place on grill. Light charcoal grill or preheat gas grill to 350° to 400° (**medium-high**). Remove chicken from marinade; discard marinade. Thread chicken and lemon wedges alternately onto skewers, leaving ⅛-inch space between pieces.

4. Grill kabobs, covered with grill lid, 6 to 8 minutes on each side or until a meat thermometer inserted into thickest portion registers 165°. Transfer to a serving platter, and sprinkle with cilantro leaves.

PRIME CHOICE

Gochujang is a Korean condiment with tons of bright, peppery flavor. It's made with chile peppers, but it's sweet enough for children.

GRILLED CHICKEN TACOS

For an easy side, combine 2 (20.5-oz.) cans refried black beans, ½ (8-oz.) package whipped chive-flavored cream cheese, and ½ tsp. ground cumin in a 2-qt. baking dish. Top with 2 Tbsp. finely chopped red onion and 1 cup crumbled queso fresco (fresh Mexican cheese). Bake at 450° for 20 to 30 minutes or until cheese melts.

SERVES 4 to 6
HANDS-ON 20 min.
TOTAL 42 min.

3   Tbsp. olive oil
2   Tbsp. fresh lime juice
4   tsp. Montreal chicken seasoning
1½ lb. chicken breast tenders
1   (8-oz.) container refrigerated fresh salsa
1   large mango, peeled and chopped
¼   cup chopped fresh cilantro
2   tsp. chipotle hot sauce
6   (6-inch) fajita-size flour tortillas, warmed
    Toppings: crumbled queso fresco (fresh Mexican cheese), shredded romaine lettuce

1. Light charcoal grill or preheat gas grill to 300° to 350° (**medium**). Combine first 3 ingredients in a zip-top plastic freezer bag; add chicken, turning to coat. Seal and chill 10 minutes, turning once.

2. Meanwhile, combine salsa and next 3 ingredients. Cover and chill until ready to serve.

3. Remove chicken from marinade; discard marinade. Grill chicken, covered with grill lid, 6 minutes on each side or until a meat thermometer inserted into thickest portion registers 165°. Serve in flour tortillas with mango salsa and desired toppings.

GRILLED BOURBON-CRANBERRY TURKEY TENDERLOIN

SERVES 4 to 6
HANDS-ON 15 min.
TOTAL 1 hr., 55 min.

Substitute apple cider for a non-alcoholic option.

1   (16-oz.) can whole-berry cranberry sauce
⅓   cup firmly packed brown sugar
⅔   cup bourbon
2   Tbsp. grated orange zest
4   lb. turkey tenderloins
1½ tsp. table salt
1   Tbsp. coarsely ground black pepper
    Garnish: grilled orange slices

1. Bring first 4 ingredients to a boil in a saucepan over medium-high heat; reduce heat to medium-low, and simmer 10 minutes or until mixture thickens slightly. Remove from heat, and let stand 30 minutes or until mixture cools to room temperature. Remove ½ cup cranberry mixture; reserve remaining mixture.

2. Rinse tenderloins, and pat dry with paper towels. Brush with ¼ cup cranberry mixture, and let stand at room temperature 30 minutes. Sprinkle with salt and pepper.

3. Light charcoal grill or preheat gas grill to 350° to 400° (**medium-high**). Grill tenderloins 10 to 12 minutes on each side or until a meat thermometer inserted into thickest portion registers 165°, basting occasionally with ¼ cup cranberry mixture. Remove from heat, and let stand 15 minutes before slicing. Serve with reserved cranberry mixture.

GRILLED TURKEY BREAST

If you don't have access to a fresh turkey breast, a frozen turkey breast, thawed, may be substituted.

SERVES 8

HANDS-ON 20 min.

TOTAL 1 hr., 35 min., plus 8 hr. for marinating

⅓ cup kosher salt

⅓ cup sugar

3 bay leaves

2 jalapeño peppers, halved

2 Tbsp. cumin seeds

1 (5- to 6-lb.) boned, skin-on fresh turkey breast
Vegetable cooking spray

1 Tbsp. table salt

1 Tbsp. cumin seeds

1 Tbsp. paprika

2 tsp. freshly ground black pepper

1 tsp. ground coriander

1 tsp. dried oregano

1. Stir together kosher salt, next 4 ingredients, and 2 qt. water in a large, deep food-safe container or stockpot until sugar dissolves. Add turkey; chill 8 hours or overnight, turning once.

2. Coat cold cooking grate with cooking spray, and place on grill. Light 1 side of charcoal grill or preheat gas grill to 350° to 400° (**medium-high**); leave other side unlit. Remove turkey from brine; discard brine. Rinse turkey, and drain well; pat dry with paper towels.

3. Stir together table salt and next 5 ingredients. Rub skin of turkey with mixture.

4. Place turkey, skin side down, over lit side of grill, and grill, without grill lid, 4 to 5 minutes or until slightly charred. Transfer to unlit side, skin side up. Grill, covered with grill lid, 30 to 40 minutes or until a meat thermometer inserted into thickest portion registers 165°. Return turkey, skin side down, to lit side, and grill, covered with grill lid, 4 to 5 minutes or until skin is crisp. Remove turkey from grill; cover loosely with aluminum foil. Let stand 10 minutes before serving.

PAPAW'S SMOKED TURKEY

SERVES 8 to 10

HANDS-ON 55 min.

TOTAL 8 hr., 10 min., plus 2 days for brining

Brining produces an extra juicy, flavorful turkey breast. It's perfect for sandwiches when thinly sliced.

1 (6- to 6½-lb.) skin-on, bone-in turkey breast
½ cup pickling salt
⅓ cup dark molasses
¼ cup Worcestershire sauce
3 Tbsp. minced garlic
1 Tbsp. freshly ground black pepper
Apple wood chips

1. Rinse turkey with cold water, and pat dry. Stir together 2 qt. water, salt, and next 4 ingredients in a 2-gal. zip-top plastic freezer bag; add turkey. Seal bag, and chill 2 days.

2. Soak wood chips in water 30 minutes. Prepare smoker according to manufacturer's directions, bringing internal temperature to 225° to 250°, maintaining temperature for 15 to 20 minutes.

3. Remove turkey from brine; discard brine. Rinse turkey under cold running water, and pat dry with paper towels. Drain wood chips, and place on coals. Place turkey on lower cooking grate; cover with smoker lid.

4. Smoke turkey, maintaining temperature inside smoker between 225° to 250°, for 6½ hours or until a meat thermometer inserted into thickest portion of turkey registers 165°; add additional charcoal and wood chips as needed. Remove turkey from smoker, and let stand 15 minutes before slicing.

ASIAN GRILLED QUAIL

The robust, umami-laden sauce brings a blast of Asian flavor to the dark, gamey poultry in this marinated quail dish.

SERVES 4

HANDS-ON 45 min.

TOTAL 1 hr., 15 min.

¼   cup hoisin sauce

2   Tbsp. sesame seeds

3   Tbsp. Asian chili-garlic sauce

3   Tbsp. dark sesame oil

3   Tbsp. honey

1   tsp. ground ginger

8   quail, dressed

1   (14-oz.) can chicken broth

2   tsp. cornstarch

Garnish: sliced green onions or green onion curls

1. Whisk together first 6 ingredients in a shallow dish or large zip-top plastic freezer bag; add quail. Cover or seal, and chill 30 minutes, turning occasionally.

2. Remove quail from marinade, reserving marinade. Light 1 side of charcoal grill or preheat gas grill to 350° to 400° (**medium-high**); leave other side unlit.

3. Place quail over unlit side, and grill, covered with grill lid, 30 minutes or until a meat thermometer inserted into thickest portion registers 165°. Pour reserved marinade into a small saucepan. Reserve ¼ cup chicken broth, and add remaining chicken broth to marinade. Bring mixture to a boil over medium-high heat; boil, stirring occasionally, 5 minutes. Whisk together cornstarch and reserved ¼ cup chicken broth until smooth. Whisk into marinade mixture; boil, whisking constantly, 1 minute. Serve with quail.

STEP-BY-STEP

1. Marinate quail for at least 30 minutes.

2. Use indirect heat to prevent quail from burning.

PIGS

COOKING OVER A FIRE is as primitive, as simple, and as basic as it gets. You do not need any professional training or experience, just an understanding of the essentials of preparing meat on a grill. It takes a glowing bed of extremely hot briquettes, a grill grid, a bag of hardwood chips, and tongs. Less can always be better than more in grilling and that rule of thumb certainly applies to the king of all meats: pork.

The vintage image of a pig has become something of a cultish symbol. Pigs appear in logos, on sides of trucks and trailers, on bumper stickers, and as mascots. Pork wins because of its natural sweetness that plays off bigger flavors in a very complementary way. Bold, acidic flavors put on some of their best performances on the pork stage. Tamarind and soy, ginger and chiles, fruity concentrates and bright vinegars—pork lets your culinary imagination run wild.

One of the pleasures of growing up in New Orleans with a dad who was raised in Cuba was his compulsion for using indigenous Cuban flavors in dishes he prepared on the grill—peasant food, comfort food, all the foods I still want to eat. Pork was the first meat of choice—especially pork tenderloin. He'd often roast or grill them whole, dousing them in amazing sauces. He created harmony by imparting a sweet, tangy depth to the earthy charred meatiness beneath. In true Cuban style, pork was never complete without a mojo, the perfect counterpoint to meat. It is a sauce of the island, made up of garlic, olive oil, and citrus juice. I am fortunate to have never been deprived of learning about my heritage and the ritual of cooking on an open flame. These lessons instilled a lifelong love of grilling pork.

Honey-and-Whole Grain
Mustard Grilled Pork Chops,
page 144

PEACH PULLED PORK

If you don't have a smoker, turn your kettle grill into one by practicing the indirect cooking method. Be sure to add more coals halfway through cooking and rotate your meat periodically.

SERVES 10
HANDS-ON 1 hr., 5 min.
TOTAL 10 hr.

Peach wood chips
1   (6¼-lb.) bone-in pork shoulder roast (Boston butt)
½   cup Cowgirl Pork Rub (page 25)
1   cup peach nectar
⅔   cup cider vinegar
1   (12-oz.) jar peach preserves

1. Soak wood chips in water 30 minutes. Prepare smoker according to manufacturer's directions, bringing internal temperature to 225° to 250° (see headnote); maintain temperature for 15 to 20 minutes. Coat roast with Cowgirl Pork Rub, pressing gently to adhere; let stand 30 minutes. Fill a spray bottle with peach nectar and 1 cup water.

2. Drain wood chips, and place on coals. Place roast on upper cooking grate; cover with smoker lid. Smoke roast, maintaining temperature inside smoker between 225° to 250°, for 8½ hours or until a meat thermometer inserted into thickest portion registers 145°, spraying occasionally with peach nectar mixture. Add additional water, charcoal, and wood chips as needed.

3. Remove roast from smoker, and let stand 15 minutes; shred or chop roast. Cook vinegar and preserves in a small saucepan over medium-low heat, stirring often, until preserves melt and mixture is smooth. Serve sauce with pork.

STEP-BY-STEP

1. Liberally coat the pork butt with rub.

2. Spraying the pork with peach nectar adds flavor and keeps the meat moist.

3. The best tool to shred pork is a pair of forks.

SMOKED PAPRIKA PORK ROAST WITH STICKY STOUT BARBECUE SAUCE

SERVES 8

HANDS-ON 25 min.

TOTAL 1 hr., 51 min., plus 1 day for marinating

This recipe calls for rubbing a salt mixture on the pork and chilling it for a day, which allows the salt to pull the other seasonings into the meat and improves the juiciness and flavor. Unlike using a "wet" marinade, you chill the meat uncovered to keep the rub "dry."

2   Tbsp. smoked paprika
2   Tbsp. brown sugar
1   Tbsp. kosher salt
1   garlic clove, pressed
1   tsp. coarsely ground black pepper

4   tsp. chopped fresh thyme, divided
1   (3½- to 4-lb.) boneless pork loin roast
    Kitchen string
    Sticky Stout Barbecue Sauce

1. Stir together first 5 ingredients and 2 tsp. thyme. Trim pork roast; rub paprika mixture over pork. Tie roast with kitchen string at 1½-inch intervals, and place in a 13- x 9-inch baking dish. Chill, uncovered, 24 hours.

2. Light 1 side of charcoal grill or preheat gas grill to 350° to 400° (**medium-high**); leave other side unlit. Place pork over lit side, and grill, covered with grill lid, 8 minutes on each side or until browned. Transfer pork to unlit side, and grill, covered with grill lid, 35 to 45 minutes or until a meat thermometer inserted in thickest portion registers 145°. Let stand 10 minutes. Brush with Sticky Stout Barbecue Sauce. Sprinkle with remaining 2 tsp. thyme, and serve with remaining barbecue sauce.

STICKY STOUT BARBECUE SAUCE

Makes: 2 cups   Hands-on: 25 min.   Total: 25 min.

1   small onion, finely chopped
1   Tbsp. vegetable oil
2   garlic cloves, minced
1   (11.2-oz.) bottle stout beer

1   cup spicy barbecue sauce
¼   cup fig preserves
2   Tbsp. cider vinegar

1. Sauté onion in hot oil in a large saucepan over medium-high heat 4 to 5 minutes or until tender. Add garlic; sauté 1 minute. Gradually stir in beer. Cook 8 to 10 minutes or until mixture is reduced by half. Reduce heat to medium; stir in barbecue sauce and next 2 ingredients, and cook 4 to 5 minutes or until thoroughly heated.

PRIME CHOICE

Smoked paprika has a distinctively robust and smoky taste made from drying and smoking sweet peppers. It adds richness and spice to any rub.

SWEET-AND-SOUR PORK TENDERLOIN

Be sure to wear gloves when seeding and mincing jalapeño peppers. The compound in chiles (called capsaicin) makes them taste spicy, but may also burn your fingers.

SERVES 4

HANDS-ON 39 min.

TOTAL 44 min.

2   Tbsp. sugar

6   Tbsp. cider vinegar

2   Tbsp. ketchup

2   Tbsp. molasses

1   Tbsp. minced garlic

1   Tbsp. seeded and minced jalapeño pepper

½   tsp. table salt

1½ tsp. minced fresh ginger

1   (1-lb.) pork tenderloin

1   Tbsp. olive oil

½   tsp. kosher salt

½   tsp. coarsely ground black pepper

1. Whisk together first 8 ingredients in a small saucepan; bring to a boil. Remove from heat, and cool 30 minutes. Reserve ¼ cup sauce to serve with cooked pork.

2. Light charcoal grill or preheat gas grill to 300° to 350° (**medium**). Remove silver skin from tenderloin, leaving a thin layer of fat. Rub pork tenderloin with oil; sprinkle with salt and pepper.

3. Grill pork, covered with grill lid, 18 minutes or until a meat thermometer inserted into thickest portion registers 145°, turning occasionally and basting often with remaining ½ cup sauce. Remove from grill, and let stand 5 minutes before slicing. Slice and serve with reserved ¼ cup sauce.

PORK TENDERLOIN SLIDERS WITH SPICY PICKLES

SERVES 16

HANDS-ON 21 min.

TOTAL 26 min.,
plus 1 day for marinating

Serve these finger-licking sandwiches on a large platter.
Be sure to have extra napkins on hand!

1 (16-oz.) jar dill pickle chips, drained
¼ cup sugar
2 tsp. chipotle hot sauce
½ tsp. dried crushed red pepper
2 (1-lb.) pork tenderloins
2 Tbsp. olive oil
1½ tsp. kosher salt
½ tsp. freshly ground black pepper
½ cup bottled sweet red barbecue sauce, divided
16 yeast rolls, split

1. Stir together first 4 ingredients in a large bowl or zip-top plastic freezer bag. Cover or seal pickle mixture, and chill 24 hours.

2. Light charcoal grill or preheat gas grill to 300° to 350° (**medium**). Rub tenderloins with oil, and sprinkle with salt and pepper. Grill tenderloins, covered with grill lid, 15 to 18 minutes or until a meat thermometer inserted into thickest portion registers 145°, turning twice and basting with ¼ cup barbecue sauce. Remove from grill; let stand 5 minutes before slicing.

3. Cut tenderloins into ½-inch-thick slices, and serve on rolls with remaining ¼ cup barbecue sauce and chilled pickles.

STEP-BY-STEP

1. Silver skin doesn't break down during grilling. Be sure to remove it from your tenderloin, leaving a layer of fat.

2. Use a silicone basting brush when basting right on the grill. Other brushes' bristles may melt.

GRILLED PORTERHOUSE PORK CHOPS WITH PEACH AGRODOLCE

SERVES 4
HANDS-ON 15 min.
TOTAL 1 hr., 25 min.

Thick-cut pork porterhouse includes a juicy portion of the tenderloin on one side and a large cut of the loin on the other.

4   (1½-inch-thick) porterhouse pork chops (about 2½ lb.)
1   Tbsp. olive oil
¾   tsp. kosher salt
½   tsp. freshly ground black pepper
    Peach Agrodolce

1. Let pork stand at room temperature 30 minutes. Light 1 side of charcoal grill or preheat gas grill to 350° to 400° (**medium-high**); leave other side unlit. Brush pork with oil, and sprinkle with salt and pepper.

2. Grill pork over lit side of grill, covered with grill lid, 4 minutes on each side. Transfer pork to unlit side, and grill, covered with grill lid, 10 minutes on each side or until a meat thermometer inserted into thickest portion registers 145°. Remove from grill, and let stand 5 minutes. Arrange pork on a serving platter, and serve with Peach Agrodolce.

PEACH AGRODOLCE

Makes: 1½ cups   Hands-on: 15 min.   Total: 15 min.

2   Tbsp. raisins
2   Tbsp. tawny port wine
1   Tbsp. chopped fresh parsley
1   Tbsp. balsamic vinegar
1   Tbsp. olive oil

2   large fresh, ripe peaches, peeled and diced into 1-inch pieces
    Kosher salt
    Freshly ground black pepper

1. Cook raisins, port, and 2 Tbsp. water in a small saucepan over medium heat, stirring occasionally, 5 minutes. Remove from heat; whisk in parsley, vinegar, and oil. Stir in peaches, and season with salt and pepper to taste.

PRIME CHOICE

Agrodolce is a traditional sweet and sour sauce typical in Italian cuisine. The term comes from "agro" which means sour, and "dolce" which means sweet.

GRILLED PORK TACOS

These lightened-up pork tacos get bright, fresh flavor from the cilantro slaw with added sweetness from pineapple tidbits. Perfect for a weeknight dinner for your family.

SERVES 6
HANDS-ON 45 min.
TOTAL 1 hr, 30 min.

6   (1-inch-thick) boneless pork chops
½   small head napa cabbage, thinly sliced (about 4 cups)
1   (8-oz.) can pineapple tidbits, drained
⅓   cup thinly sliced green onions
⅓   cup chopped radishes (about 2 large)
¼   cup thinly sliced sweet onion
¼   cup shredded carrot
¼   cup finely chopped fresh cilantro
2   Tbsp. Champagne vinegar
3   Tbsp. olive oil, divided
1   tsp. kosher salt
½   tsp. freshly ground black pepper
12   (6-inch) fajita-size flour tortillas
    Lime wedges

1. Let pork chops stand at room temperature 30 to 40 minutes. Meanwhile, mix next 8 ingredients together in a medium bowl. Add 1 tablespoon olive oil, and season with salt and pepper to taste. Cover and chill 30 minutes.

2. Light 1 side of charcoal grill or preheat gas grill to 350° to 400° (**medium-high**); leave other side unlit. Brush pork with remaining olive oil, and sprinkle with 1 tsp. salt and ½ tsp. pepper. Grill pork chops over lit side of grill, covered with grill lid, 4 minutes on each side; transfer pork to unlit side, and grill, covered with grill lid, 10 minutes on each side or until a meat thermometer inserted into thickest portion registers 145°. Let stand 5 minutes. Thinly slice pork.

3. Place sliced pork in warm tortillas; top with cilantro slaw. Serve with lime wedges.

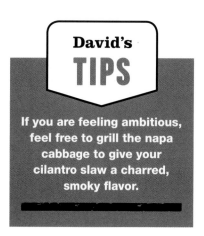

David's
TIPS

If you are feeling ambitious, feel free to grill the napa cabbage to give your cilantro slaw a charred, smoky flavor.

HONEY-AND-WHOLE GRAIN MUSTARD-GRILLED PORK CHOPS

SERVES 4

HANDS-ON 24 min.

TOTAL 2 hr., 24 min.,
plus 6 hr. for marinating

Of all the condiments I own, honey and mustard are most certainly the ones that have a dominating presence in my pantry. Over the years, I've become something of a collector. At any given time, I'll have more than a dozen mustards and 30 or 40 honeys scattered about my kitchen. I prefer to cook with whole grain mustard for its bold flavor, snappy taste, and gritty texture.

¾   cup kosher salt

¾   cup honey, divided

1   cup hot water

3   cups plus 2 Tbsp. cold water, divided

4   (12- to 14-oz.) bone-in, double-cut pork chops

¼   cup Creole mustard

2   Tbsp. olive oil

1. Combine salt, ½ cup honey, and 1 cup hot water in an 8-qt. container; whisk until salt and honey dissolve. Whisk in 3 cups cold water, and add pork chops. Cover and refrigerate 6 to 8 hours.

2. Light charcoal grill or preheat gas grill to 350° to 400° (**medium-high**). Remove pork chops from brine; rinse under cold water, and pat dry with paper towels. Combine mustard, remaining ¼ cup honey, and 1 Tbsp. cold water in a small bowl.

3. Pour olive oil into a large cast-iron skillet; place on grill grate and heat until hot. Add pork chops, and sear 2 minutes. Turn pork chops, and brush with mustard-honey mixture, reserving remaining mixture; close grill lid, and cook 15 to 20 minutes or until a meat thermometer inserted into thickest portion registers 145°. Remove pork chops from oven, and place, glazed sides down, on a cutting board; let stand.

4. Remove skillet from grill; add remaining mustard-honey mixture and remaining 1 Tbsp. cold water. Cook, stirring with a wooden spoon to loosen browned bits from bottom of skillet, 1 to 2 minutes or until mixture thickens. Cut each pork chop into 5 to 6 slices, and place in a fanlike shape on serving platter; brush or drizzle glaze over top.

SLOW-GRILLED PORK WITH RANCH BARBECUE SAUCE

1   (1-oz.) envelope Ranch dressing mix
1   (5-lb.) bone-in pork shoulder roast (Boston butt)
½   (16-oz.) bottle Creole butter injection marinade (with injector)
     Ranch-Barbecue Sauce

SERVES 6
HANDS-ON 15 min.
TOTAL 4 hr., plus
8 hr. for marinating

1. Rub dressing mix evenly over roast. Wrap tightly with plastic wrap, and place in a shallow dish or large zip-top plastic freezer bag; cover or seal, and chill 8 hours. Let stand at room temperature 30 minutes before grilling. Remove plastic wrap.

2. Light 1 side of charcoal grill or preheat gas grill to 400° to 500° (**high**); leave other side unlit. Place roast, fat side up, over unlit side of grill, and grill, covered with grill lid, 3½ to 4½ hours or until meat thermometer inserted into thickest portion registers 145°. (Meat will easily pull away from bone.) Let stand 15 minutes. Coarsely chop, and serve with Ranch-Barbecue Sauce.

RANCH-BARBECUE SAUCE

Makes: 1¼ cups   Hands-on: 5 min.   Total: 20 min.

1   (18-oz.) bottle barbecue sauce
1   (1-oz.) envelope Ranch dressing mix
¼   cup honey
½   tsp. dry mustard

1. Stir together all ingredients in a saucepan over medium-high heat; bring to a boil. Reduce heat, and simmer, stirring occasionally, 20 minutes.

SPINACH SALAD WITH GRILLED PORK TENDERLOIN AND NECTARINES

SERVES 6
HANDS-ON 6 min.
TOTAL 16 min.

Grilling heightens the sweetness and flavor of the nectarines. Because they have such thin skins, nectarines don't require peeling for this dish. However, you may substitute fresh peeled peaches if you prefer.

1 (1-lb.) peppercorn-flavored pork tenderloin, trimmed
3 nectarines, halved
   Vegetable cooking spray
2 (6-oz.) packages fresh baby spinach
¼ cup light balsamic vinaigrette
¼ cup (1 oz.) crumbled feta cheese
   Freshly ground black pepper (optional)

1. Light charcoal grill or preheat gas grill to 300° to 350° (**medium**). Cut pork horizontally through center of meat, cutting to, but not through, other side using a sharp knife; open flat as you would a book. Place pork and nectarine halves, cut sides down, on grill grate coated with cooking spray.

2. Grill pork 5 minutes on each side or until a meat thermometer inserted into thickest portion registers 145°. Grill nectarine halves 4 to 5 minutes on each side or until thoroughly heated. Remove pork and nectarine halves from grill. Let pork rest 10 minutes.

3. Cut nectarine halves into slices. Thinly slice pork. Combine spinach and vinaigrette in a large bowl; toss gently to coat.

4. Divide spinach mixture evenly on 6 plates. Top each serving evenly with nectarine slices and pork slices. Sprinkle with cheese. Sprinkle evenly with pepper, if desired.

PRIME CHOICE

Look for the peppercorn-flavored pork tenderloin with other shrink-wrapped meat at your local grocer.

CIDER-BRINED GRILLED PORK CHOPS

Grilled pork chops benefit dramatically from a hard cider brine that penetrates right to the middle of the meat and an apple-brandy glaze that coats the outside of the pork with tangy sweetness.

SERVES 6

HANDS-ON 15 min.

TOTAL 1 hr., 40 min.

BRINE:

1½ cups hard apple cider

½ cup kosher salt

1 Tbsp. dried rosemary

1 Tbsp. dried sage

1½ tsp. dried thyme

½ tsp. whole black peppercorns

PORK:

4 center-cut pork loin chops, each about 12 oz. and 1½ inches thick, trimmed of excess fat

Extra virgin olive oil

GLAZE:

6 Tbsp. apple jelly

2 Tbsp. unsalted butter

2 Tbsp. Calvados or applejack (apple brandy)

GRILLED APPLES:

4 Granny Smith apples, each cut into 6 wedges and cores removed

1. Combine brine ingredients in a large bowl. Put the chops in a large zip-top plastic bag, and pour in the brine. Press the air out of the bag, and seal tightly. Place the bag in a bowl or a rimmed dish, and refrigerate for 1 to 1½ hours, turning bag every 30 minutes.

2. Remove the chops from the bag; discard brine. Rinse chops under cold water; pat dry with paper towels. Lightly brush or spray chops with oil; let stand at room temperature for 20 to 30 minutes before grilling.

3. In a small saucepan over medium-low heat, warm jelly and butter, stirring until jelly melts. Remove from heat, and stir in Calvados (reheat gently, if needed). Set aside half of glaze to serve as a sauce with the pork. Brush remaining glaze over apple wedges and then over chops.

4. Light charcoal grill or preheat gas grill to 300° to 350° (**medium**). Brush chops with oil, and grill over direct heat, covered with grill lid, 5 minutes on each side or until a meat thermometer inserted into thickest portion registers 145°. Remove chops from grill, and let rest for 3 to 5 minutes. Grill apples over direct heat 1 minute on each side or until crisp-tender. Serve chops and apples with reserved glaze.

PRIME CHOICE

Hard apple cider is a fermented alcoholic drink made from unfiltered apple juice. It has a distinctive sweet-tart taste.

BROWN SUGAR PORK CHOPS WITH PEACH BARBECUE SAUCE

SERVES 4
HANDS-ON 45 min.
TOTAL 1 hr., 20 min.

The sugar in the barbecue sauce can burn, which is why basting at the end of grilling is key.

¾ cup firmly packed dark brown sugar

¼ cup kosher salt

2 cups boiling water

3 cups ice cubes

4 bone-in pork loin chops (about 2 lb.)

1 medium-size sweet onion, finely chopped

1 Tbsp. canola oil

1 garlic clove, minced

1 (1-inch) piece fresh ginger, peeled and grated

1½ cups ketchup

½ cup peach preserves or jam

2 large peaches (about 1 lb.), peeled and cut into ¾-inch chunks

2 Tbsp. cider vinegar

Kosher salt

Freshly ground black pepper

Garnish: fresh oregano sprigs

1. Combine sugar and salt in a large bowl; add boiling water, stirring until sugar and salt dissolve. Stir in ice cubes to cool mixture. Add pork chops; cover and chill 30 minutes.

2. Meanwhile, sauté onion in hot oil in a medium saucepan over medium heat 2 minutes or until tender. Add garlic and ginger; cook, stirring constantly, 45 to 60 seconds or until fragrant. Add ketchup, peach preserves, and peaches. Reduce heat to low, and simmer, stirring occasionally, 30 minutes or until sauce thickens. Add vinegar; season with salt and pepper to taste. Remove from heat.

3. Remove pork from brine; discard brine. Rinse pork well, and pat dry with paper towels.

4. Light charcoal grill or preheat gas grill to 350° to 400° (**medium-high**). Pour half of peach mixture into a bowl; reserve remaining peach mixture. Season both sides of pork with desired amount of salt and pepper.

5. Grill pork, covered with grill lid, 5 to 6 minutes on each side or until a meat thermometer inserted into thickest portion registers 145°, basting pork occasionally with peach mixture in bowl. Remove pork from grill; let stand 5 minutes before serving. Serve with reserved peach mixture.

PEACH-GLAZED PORK CHOPS

Serve this summery meal with a lightly dressed salad and a refreshingly cool iced tea.

SERVES 4

HANDS-ON 31 min.

TOTAL 36 min.

1   (18-oz.) jar peach preserves
¼   cup soy sauce
2   Tbsp. grated fresh ginger
2   tsp. olive oil
4   (8-oz.) bone-in pork loin chops (1½ inches thick)
¼   tsp. table salt
¼   tsp. freshly ground black pepper
4   large peaches, halved

1. Light charcoal grill or preheat gas grill to 350° to 400° (**medium-high**). Bring preserves, soy sauce, and ginger to a boil in a small saucepan. Remove from heat; reserve ½ cup to baste peaches.

2. Rub oil over pork chops; sprinkle with salt and pepper. Grill pork chops, covered with grill lid, 5 to 7 minutes on each side or until a meat thermometer inserted into thickest portion registers 145°, basting often with 1 cup peach preserves mixture.

3. At the same time, grill peaches, covered with grill lid, 2 to 3 minutes on each side or until tender, basting often with reserved ½ cup peach preserves mixture. Let pork chops stand 5 minutes before serving with peaches.

PRIME CHOICE

Peach preserves are preferable for this recipe, but if you only have apricot or orange preserves on hand, they also impart a sweet and tangy flavor.

WHISKEY-MARINATED PORK TENDERLOIN

Pork tenderloin should be served slightly pink in the center, so check the time closely. It shouldn't take more than 16 to 18 minutes to reach 145°; then cover the pork, and let it stand while you boil the marinade to serve as a sauce.

SERVES 4
HANDS-ON 25 min.
TOTAL 2 hr., 35 min.

1 (1-lb.) pork tenderloin
6 Tbsp. Worcestershire sauce
3 Tbsp. bourbon or whiskey
3 Tbsp. maple syrup
2 Tbsp. honey-Dijon mustard
2 Tbsp. olive oil
¼ tsp. freshly ground black pepper
½ tsp. table salt

1. Remove silver skin from tenderloin, leaving a thin layer of fat.

2. Whisk together Worcestershire sauce and next 5 ingredients in a small bowl until blended. Pour marinade into a large shallow dish or zip-top plastic freezer bag; add pork, cover or seal, and chill 2 hours, turning occasionally. Remove pork, reserving marinade. Sprinkle pork with salt.

3. Light charcoal grill or preheat gas grill to 350° to 400° (**medium-high**). Grill tenderloin, covered with grill lid, 8 to 9 minutes on each side or until a meat thermometer inserted into thickest portion registers 145°. Remove from grill, and let stand 10 minutes before slicing.

4. Meanwhile, bring reserved marinade to a boil in a small saucepan over medium-high heat; boil, stirring occasionally, 2 minutes. Serve with sliced pork.

David's
TIPS

The bourbon or whiskey in the marinade acts as a tenderizer, not a flavor enhancer. So, there's no need to use your good stuff in this application.

PINEAPPLE GRILLED PORK TENDERLOIN

SERVES 6 to 8
HANDS-ON 18 min.
TOTAL 48 min.

This Hawaiian-inspired dish pairs perfectly with sticky rice and steamed snow peas.

2   (1-lb.) pork tenderloins
1   tsp. table salt
½   tsp. freshly ground black pepper
1   (8-oz.) can pineapple slices in juice
2   limes
¼   cup orange marmalade
3   Tbsp. hoisin sauce
3   Tbsp. soy sauce
2   garlic cloves, pressed
1   tsp. Dijon mustard
½   tsp. ground ginger

1. Light charcoal grill or preheat gas grill to 350° to 400° (**medium-high**). Remove silver skin from tenderloins, leaving a thin layer of fat. Sprinkle pork with salt and pepper.

2. Drain pineapple, reserving ⅓ cup juice. Grate zest from limes to equal 1 Tbsp.; squeeze juice from limes to equal ⅓ cup.

3. Bring reserved ⅓ cup pineapple juice, lime juice, zest, marmalade, and next 5 ingredients to a boil in a saucepan over medium-high heat. Boil 3 to 4 minutes or until slightly thickened. Reserve half of pineapple mixture in a bowl to serve with pork.

4. Grill pork, covered with grill lid, 10 to 12 minutes on each side or until a meat thermometer inserted into thickest portion registers 145°, basting with remaining pineapple mixture. Remove from grill; cover with aluminum foil, and let stand 10 minutes before serving with pineapple slices.

SPICY GRILLED PORK TENDERLOIN WITH BLACKBERRY SAUCE

Jerk seasoning provides the heat in this spicy dish, while the sweet blackberry sauce keeps the flavor from going over the top.

SERVES 6 to 8
HANDS-ON 15 min.
TOTAL 45 min.

2   (¾-lb.) pork tenderloins
1   Tbsp. olive oil
1½ Tbsp. Caribbean jerk seasoning
1   tsp. table salt
⅔   cup seedless blackberry preserves
¼   cup Dijon mustard
2   Tbsp. rum or orange juice
1   Tbsp. orange zest
1   Tbsp. grated fresh ginger

1. Light charcoal grill or preheat gas grill to 350° to 400° (**medium-high**). Remove silver skin from tenderloins, leaving a thin layer of fat. Brush tenderloins with oil, and rub with seasoning and salt.

2. Grill tenderloins, covered with grill lid, 10 minutes on each side or until a meat thermometer inserted into thickest portion registers 145°. Remove from grill, and let stand 10 minutes.

3. Meanwhile, whisk together blackberry preserves and next 4 ingredients in a small saucepan, and cook over low heat, whisking constantly, 5 minutes or until thoroughly heated.

4. Cut pork diagonally into thin slices, and arrange on a serving platter; drizzle with warm sauce.

GRILL SMOKED PORK TENDERLOIN WITH GUAVA BBQ SAUCE

SERVES 6

HANDS-ON 45 min.

TOTAL 45 min., plus 6 hr. for marinating

If using a gas grill, place wood chips in aluminum foil and gently fold up sides leaving some open space.

¾ cup kosher salt	Kosher salt
¼ cup sugar	Cracked black pepper
1 cup hot water	Sweet and Spicy Guava Barbecue Sauce, divided
3 cups cold water	
1 (2-lb.) pork tenderloin	1 cup apple wood chips, soaked in water
Olive oil	

1. Combine salt, sugar, and 1 cup hot water in an 8-qt. container; whisk until salt and sugar dissolve. Whisk in 3 cups cold water; add tenderloin. Cover and refrigerate 6 to 8 hours. About 1 hour before grilling, light 1 side of charcoal grill or preheat gas grill to 350° to 400° (**medium-high**); leave other side unlit.

2. Remove tenderloin from brine; rinse under cold water, and pat dry with paper towels. Brush with olive oil, and season with salt and pepper. Place on cooking grate over lit coals; grill 5 minutes on each side. Liberally brush with Sweet and Spicy Guava Barbecue Sauce, and move to unlit side of grill. Sprinkle wood chips over lit coals (or place foil packet on gas grill); cover with grill lid, and grill, basting tenderloin every 5 minutes with sauce, 20 minutes or until a meat thermometer inserted into thickest portion registers 145°.

3. Remove tenderloin from grill; brush with remaining sauce. Place on cutting board; let stand 15 minutes before slicing and serving.

SWEET AND SPICY GUAVA BARBECUE SAUCE

Makes: 2 cups   Hands-on: 10 min.   Total: 10 min.

12 oz. guava paste, cubed	4 Tbsp. cane syrup
½ cup orange juice	2 Tbsp. Creole mustard
¼ cup dark rum	1 Tbsp. hot sauce
¼ cup lime juice	1 tsp. kosher salt
2 garlic cloves, minced	½ tsp. crushed red pepper

1. Combine all ingredients in a 2-qt. saucepan over low heat. Simmer, stirring occasionally with a wooden spoon, 10 minutes or until guava paste dissolves and mixture thickens.

David's TIPS

When we'd have an open tin of guava paste in the house, we'd put slices of it on big white airy crackers, or *galletas*, with salty *Manchego* cheese. It's a classic Cuban snack— simple and addictive.

APPLE-KALE STUFFED PORK LOIN

- 1 (3½-lb.) boneless pork loin
- ¼ cup firmly packed light brown sugar
- ¼ cup yellow mustard
- ¼ cup red wine vinegar
- 2 Tbsp. All-Purpose BBQ Rub (page 22)
- 2 Tbsp. canola oil
- 1 tsp. table salt, divided
- 1 tsp. freshly ground black pepper, divided
- 6 bacon slices
- 1 Granny Smith apple, peeled and chopped
- 1 small onion, chopped
- 3 cups chopped fresh kale
- 2 Tbsp. cider vinegar
- Kitchen string

SERVES 8 to 10

HANDS-ON 25 min.

TOTAL 2 hr., 30 min., plus 8 hr. for marinating

1. Butterfly pork loin by making a horizontal cut (about one-third down from top) into 1 side of pork, cutting to within ½ inch of other side. (Do not cut all the way through roast.) Unfold top cut piece, open, and lay flat. Butterfly and repeat procedure on opposite side of remaining two-thirds portion of pork loin, beginning at top or bottom of inside cut. Place between 2 sheets of heavy-duty plastic wrap; flatten to 1-inch thickness, using a rolling pin or flat side of a meat mallet.

2. Whisk together brown sugar and next 4 ingredients in a small bowl. Pour marinade into a large zip-top plastic freezer bag; add pork, turning to coat. Seal and chill 8 to 24 hours, turning occasionally.

3. Remove pork from marinade; discard marinade. Lay pork flat on work surface; sprinkle with ½ tsp. salt and ½ tsp. pepper. Light 1 side of charcoal grill or preheat gas grill to 350° to 400° (**medium-high**); leave other side unlit.

4. Cook bacon in a large skillet over medium-high heat 5 minutes; remove bacon, and drain on paper towels, reserving 2 Tbsp. drippings in skillet. Crumble bacon. Sauté apple, onion, and kale in hot drippings 10 minutes or until tender. Add vinegar, stirring to loosen particles from bottom of skillet. Remove from heat; stir in bacon and remaining salt and pepper. Spread kale mixture over pork, leaving a ½-inch border. Roll up, starting at 1 long side, and tie with kitchen string, securing at 2-inch intervals.

5. Place stuffed pork over lit side of grill, and grill, covered with lid, 5 minutes on each side. Transfer to unlit side; grill, covered with grill lid, 1 hour and 30 minutes or until a meat thermometer registers 145°. Remove from grill; let stand 10 minutes before slicing.

STEP-BY-STEP

1. Use a boning knife to butterfly the pork loin to lay flat.

2. A meat pounder is the best tool to use to flatten the pork evenly.

MAPLE MUSTARD PORK LOIN

SERVES 10 to 12
HANDS-ON 50 min.
TOTAL 55 min.

This is a big cut of meat, so let it stand at room temperature for 30 minutes before grilling to reduce the overall cooking time.

1   (4¾-lb.) boneless pork loin
3   Tbsp. olive oil
½   tsp. table salt
¼   tsp. freshly ground black pepper
1   cup maple syrup
⅓   cup Dijon mustard
3   Tbsp. cider vinegar
3   Tbsp. soy sauce
    Pinch of table salt
    Pinch of freshly ground black pepper

1. Light charcoal grill or preheat gas grill to 300° to 350° (**medium**). Rub pork loin with oil, and sprinkle with ½ tsp. salt and ¼ tsp. pepper.

2. Stir together maple syrup and next 5 ingredients in a small bowl; reserve ½ cup syrup mixture to serve with cooked pork.

3. Grill pork, covered with grill lid, 45 minutes or until a meat thermometer inserted into thickest portion registers 145°, turning every 10 minutes and basting with remaining syrup mixture. Remove from grill, and let stand 5 minutes before slicing. Serve with reserved ½ cup syrup mixture.

EAST CAROLINA COUNTRY-STYLE RIBS

Keep those tomatoes away! Eastern Carolina barbecue is known for its puckery vinegar- and pepper-based sauces. You won't see any molasses or ketchup near this sauce.

SERVES 6
HANDS-ON 43 min.
TOTAL 1 hr., 13 min.

4   lb. bone-in country-style pork ribs
⅓   cup Pork Dry Rub (page 25)
2   cups Eastern Carolina
     Vinegar Sauce (page 22), divided

1. Sprinkle ribs with Pork Dry Rub; let stand 10 minutes. Fill a spray bottle with ½ cup East Carolina Vinegar Sauce.

2. Light charcoal grill or preheat gas grill to 400° to 450° (**high**). Grill ribs, covered with grill lid, 5 minutes on each side to sear. Reduce grill temperature to 250° to 300° (**low**). Grill, covered with grill lid, 15 minutes on each side, spraying occasionally with vinegar sauce.

3. Turn off 1 side of grill. Arrange ribs over unlit side, and grill, covered with grill lid, 30 minutes or until a meat thermometer inserted into thickest portion registers 145°, spraying with vinegar sauce occasionally. Let stand 10 minutes before serving. Serve with remaining 1½ cups vinegar sauce.

CHAMPIONSHIP GLAZED RIBS

SERVES 6

HANDS-ON 40 min.

TOTAL 5 hr.

Homemade rub with smoked paprika and a pile of apple-wood chips in the grill infuse these tender, fall-off-the-bone ribs with a thick, smoky flavor.

2   slabs pork spare ribs (about 7½ lb.)

1   cup bottled hickory and brown sugar barbecue sauce

⅓   cup honey

⅔   cup Pork Dry Rub (page 25)
    Apple wood chips, soaked in water

1. Cut slabs perpendicular to the rib bones, reserving rib tips for another use. (This style of ribs is known as the St. Louis cut. You can also have your butcher trim them for you.)

2. Remove thin membrane from back of ribs by slicing into it with a knife, and then pulling it off.

3. Stir together barbecue sauce and honey in a small bowl; reserve ½ cup to serve with cooked ribs. Sprinkle both sides of ribs generously with Pork Dry Rub; let stand 10 minutes.

4. Light 1 side of charcoal grill or preheat gas grill to 250° to 300° (**low**); leave other side unlit. Add soaked wood chips to coals. Place ribs over unlit side, and grill, covered with grill lid, 2 hours and 15 minutes.

5. Turn rib slabs over; grill 2 hours and 15 minutes or until tender and a meat thermometer inserted into thickest portion registers 145°. Cook ribs 15 more minutes, basting frequently with barbecue sauce mixture.

6. Remove ribs from grill, and let stand 10 minutes. Cut ribs, slicing between bones. Serve ribs with reserved ½ cup barbecue sauce mixture.

STEP-BY-STEP

1. Use a knife to score the membrane on the back of each rib rack.

2. Pull the membrane off slowly, using your hands or a paper towel. It should come off in a single piece.

ITALIAN GRILLED PORK SANDWICHES

SERVES 6
HANDS-ON 25 min.
TOTAL 3 hr., 58 min.

Turn this sandwich into a dinner by serving it without the hoagie roll and adding another side, such as grilled potatoes, to accompany the hearty dish.

2   Tbsp. minced garlic, divided
1½ Tbsp. finely chopped fresh rosemary
7   Tbsp. extra virgin olive oil, divided
1   Tbsp. kosher salt
2   tsp. freshly ground black pepper
1   (2¾-lb.) boneless pork loin
1   bunch broccoli rabe (rapini)
½   tsp. dried crushed red pepper
12 (0.6-oz.) smoked provolone cheese slices
6   hoagie rolls, split

1. Stir together 1½ Tbsp. garlic, rosemary, 3 Tbsp. oil, salt, and pepper in a small bowl. Place pork in a baking dish; rub pork with garlic mixture. Cover and chill at least 2 hours. Let pork stand at room temperature 45 minutes.

2. Meanwhile, light 1 side of charcoal grill or preheat gas grill to 350° to 400° (**medium-high**); leave other side unlit. Place pork over lit side, and grill, covered with grill lid, 4 minutes, turning often. Transfer pork to unlit side of grill, and grill, covered with grill lid, 30 minutes or until a meat thermometer inserted into thickest portion registers 145°. Remove from grill, and let stand 5 minutes before slicing.

3. Remove florets from broccoli rabe; trim and discard ½ inch of stem from bottom. Cook leaves and stems in boiling water 2 minutes; add florets, and cook 5 more minutes. Drain, reserving ½ cup cooking water, and plunge into an ice-water bath.

4. Heat remaining 4 Tbsp. oil in a large skillet over medium heat. Add remaining garlic and red pepper; sauté 1 minute. Add broccoli rabe; sauté 5 minutes. Add reserved ½ cup cooking water; cook 2 more minutes. Arrange 2 cheese slices on bottom halves or rolls; top with pork, broccoli rabe, and top of rolls.

PRIME CHOICE

Broccoli rabe (rapini) is particularly associated with Italian cuisine and has a slightly bitter taste.

COW AND GAME

IN MY WORLD OF GRILLING it's customary that fathers teach their sons how to prepare the meat. My Cuban grandfather (*abuelo*) taught my father the important skills of cooking impressive cuts of meat over the glowing embers, and my father translated this to me. It's now my turn to pass the torch to my sons. My boys and I are partial to skirt and hanger steaks. These long, flat cuts offer the best of what some other more expensive steaks have without breaking the bank. Skirt and hanger steaks have a higher percentage of fat and a well-developed muscle that provides rich, deep flavor. A hanger steak requires a little more time on the grill to take it past the point of the endless chewiness—there's an easy grilled bison hanger steak recipe in this chapter on page 184 that's a great place to start—while a skirt steak needs just a quick sear on the grill to lock in the flavor and keep it moist. Flank steak is unbeatable for fajitas or carne asada. My dad used to cook flank steaks more than any other cut.

Come Easter, lamb was the customary centerpiece of the Sunday celebration. This is no-frills eating to others, but to our family it was tradition, stemming from my father's Cuban heritage. The earthy meat creates a bridge between the dinner, the farmer, and the land, and the way my dad prepared it you could taste all of this in every bite. I remember watching him as he methodically cut slits all around the piece of meat, which he'd stuff to capacity with cloves of fresh garlic and sprigs of rosemary. The best part was when he carved it off the bone at the table and the skin was salty and crisp with just enough fat to have the meat remain tender so it just fell off, right onto the fork, so delicately.

Creole-Rubbed Bone-In
Rib-Eye Steaks, page 170

CREOLE-RUBBED BONE-IN RIB-EYE STEAKS

SERVES 4
HANDS-ON 28 min.
TOTAL 38 min.

In Louisiana, Tony Chachere's Creole Seasoning is a necessary pantry staple. It's not used as much as a seasoning for simmering sauces and stews as it is for dry rubs. As I became a more conscientious cook, I developed my own lower-sodium version of Creole seasoning that I always have around. The heat in the seasoning cuts through the fatty rib-eye, and the coffee adds a depth and richness to the steak's flavor.

¼   cup olive oil

6   Tbsp. ground coffee

1   Tbsp. light brown sugar

2   Tbsp. paprika

1½ Tbsp. coarse sea salt

2   tsp. granulated onion

2   tsp. granulated garlic

1   tsp. freshly ground black pepper

½   tsp. ground red pepper

4   (18- to 20-oz.) bone-in rib-eye steaks
    Coal-Roasted Garlic Compound Butter (page 28), at room temperature

1. Light charcoal grill or preheat gas grill to 350° to 400° (**medium-high**). Combine first 9 ingredients in a bowl, and brush on both sides of steaks.

2. Place steaks on cooking grate, and grill 6 to 9 minutes on each side or until desired degree of doneness.

3. Remove steaks from grill, and place on a cutting board; let stand 8 to 10 minutes. Place a dollop of Coal-Roasted Garlic Compound Butter on each steak before slicing and serving.

David's
TIPS

To avoid burning the bone before the meat is cooked, wrap it in foil to protect it from direct contact with the flames.

GRILLED STEAK-CORN-SPINACH SALAD

This salad features creamy avocado slices, grapefruit, and garlic. Add grilled steak and corn, and it's a meal your whole family will love.

1   (2-lb.) rib-eye steak
4   Tbsp. olive oil
4   garlic cloves, pressed
1¼ tsp. table salt
½   tsp. freshly ground black pepper
4   ears fresh corn, husks removed
1   (5-oz.) package fresh baby spinach
2   ripe avocados, thinly sliced
1   red grapefruit, sectioned
    Bottled peppercorn Ranch dressing

SERVES 6
HANDS-ON 30 min.
TOTAL 30 min.

1. Light charcoal grill or preheat gas grill to 350° to 400° (**medium-high**). Rub steak with 2 Tbsp. oil and next 3 ingredients. Brush corn with remaining 2 Tbsp. oil.

2. Grill steak and corn at the same time, covered with grill lid, 7 to 8 minutes, turning steak once and turning corn every 4 to 5 minutes. Let steak stand 10 minutes.

3. Meanwhile, hold each grilled cob upright on a cutting board, and carefully cut downward, cutting kernels from cob; discard cobs. Thinly slice steak.

4. Layer spinach, grilled corn kernels, steak, avocados, and grapefruit on individual plates. Serve with bottled Ranch dressing.

STEAKHOUSE SIRLOIN STEAK

SERVES 4

HANDS-ON 10 min.

TOTAL 32 min., plus 4 hr. for marinating

The length of marinating time depends on the size and cut of the beef. Let stand 30 minutes at room temperature to impart flavor, and then grill.

1 (1-lb.) boneless sirloin steak

½ cup dark beer

2 Tbsp. olive oil

1 Tbsp. Worcestershire sauce

1 Tbsp. steak sauce

1 tsp. lemon zest

½ tsp. table salt

¼ tsp. freshly ground black pepper

1. Pierce steak several times with a fork. Whisk together beer and next 6 ingredients in a shallow dish or large zip-top plastic freezer bag until blended; add steak. Cover or seal; chill at least 4 hours or up to 6 hours, turning occasionally.

2. Light charcoal grill or preheat gas grill to 350° to 400° (**medium-high**). Remove steak from marinade, discarding marinade. Pat steak dry, and sprinkle with salt and pepper.

3. Grill steak, covered with grill lid, 4 minutes on each side or until desired degree of doneness. Let stand 10 minutes before slicing.

GRILLED RIB-EYE STEAKS WITH BÉARNAISE BUTTER AND ONION RELISH

8 (14-oz.) rib-eye steaks

3½ tsp. kosher salt

1½ tsp. freshly ground white pepper

8 Tbsp. roasted cacao nibs, finely ground

Béarnaise Butter, softened

Onion Relish

SERVES 8

HANDS-ON 20 min.

TOTAL 2 hr., 23 min.

1. Season steaks with salt and pepper. Rub ground cacao nibs on both sides of steaks (about 1½ tsp. each). Let steaks stand at room temperature 30 minutes.

2. Light charcoal grill or preheat gas grill to 350° to 400° (**medium-high**). Grill steaks, covered with grill lid, 6 to 9 minutes on each side or until desired degree of doneness. Loosely cover with aluminum foil, and let stand 10 minutes. Serve with Béarnaise Butter and Onion Relish.

BÉARNAISE BUTTER

Makes: 1 cup   Hands-on: 5 min.   Total: 10 min.

1 cup butter, softened

2 Tbsp. pickled shallots, minced

1½ Tbsp. chopped fresh tarragon

¼ tsp. freshly ground black pepper

1. Beat butter, pickled shallots, tarragon, and pepper at medium speed with an electric mixer until combined. Spoon butter onto plastic wrap; roll tightly, forming a log. Serve immediately, or chill until ready to serve. Refrigerate in an airtight container up to 2 weeks.

ONION RELISH

Makes: 3 cups   Hands-on: 20 min.   Total: 1 hr., 30 min.

5 yellow onions, finely diced

1 cup sugar

2 cups white wine vinegar

1 fresh bay leaf

1 tsp. kosher salt

1 tsp. yellow mustard seeds

1 tsp. coriander seeds

½ tsp. freshly ground black pepper

1. Bring all ingredients to a boil in a heavy saucepan over high heat, stirring often. Reduce heat to medium-high, and simmer, stirring often, 30 minutes or until liquid is reduced by half and mixture reaches a syrup-like consistency. Discard bay leaf. Cool to room temperature (about 45 minutes) before serving.

PRIME CHOICE

Made from crushed cocao beans, cacao nibs resemble unsweetened chocolate chips. They are extremely flavorful and pack a punch of rich chocolate notes.

BULGOGI FLANK STEAK

The long marinating time ensures flavorful, tender bites.

½   cup soy sauce
¼   cup firmly packed light brown sugar
¼   cup chopped green onions
¼   cup dark sesame oil
2   Tbsp. dry sherry
2   Tbsp. minced fresh garlic
1   Tbsp. grated fresh ginger
1   tsp. dried crushed red pepper
1   (2-lb.) flank steak

SERVES 6
HANDS-ON 35 min.
TOTAL 45 min., plus 12 hr.
for marinating

1. Stir together first 8 ingredients in a large shallow dish or 2-gal. zip-top plastic freezer bag; add steak. Cover or seal, and chill 12 hours. Remove steak from marinade; discard marinade.

2. Light charcoal grill or preheat gas grill to 400° to 450° (**high**). Grill steak, covered with grill lid, 9 minutes on each side or until desired degree of doneness. Let stand 10 minutes. Cut diagonally across the grain into thin slices. Sprinkle with salt and pepper to taste.

PRIME CHOICE

Bulgogi is a traditional Korean dish made from marinated beef that is grilled over a very hot fire.

GRILLED MOLASSES FLANK STEAK WITH WATERMELON SALSA

SERVES 6 to 8
HANDS-ON 30 min.
TOTAL 58 min., plus 4 hr. for marinating

Serve this bright and summery main dish with a cool, creamy potato salad.

¾	cup molasses	2	Tbsp. grated fresh ginger
⅓	cup soy sauce	3	garlic cloves, minced
¼	cup canola oil	1	tsp. dried crushed red pepper
¼	cup fresh lemon juice	1	(2-lb.) flank steak
2	Tbsp. Worcestershire sauce		Watermelon Salsa

1. Stir together first 8 ingredients in a large shallow dish or 2-gal. zip-top plastic freezer bag; add steak, turning to coat. Cover or seal, and chill 4 to 12 hours. Remove steak from marinade; discard marinade.

2. Light charcoal grill or preheat gas grill to 400° to 450° (**high**). Grill steak, covered with grill lid, 9 minutes on each side or until desired degree of doneness. Remove from grill, and let stand 10 minutes. Cut diagonally across the grain into thin slices. Season with salt and pepper to taste. Top with Watermelon Salsa.

WATERMELON SALSA

Makes: about 4 cups   Hands-on: 20 min.   Total: 35 min.

1	cup diced unpeeled nectarine	2	tsp. grated fresh ginger
2	jalapeño peppers, seeded and minced	2	cups seeded and diced watermelon
1	Tbsp. sugar	½	cup chopped fresh cilantro
3	Tbsp, fresh lime juice	⅓	cup diced red onion
2	tsp. orange zest		

1. Stir together first 6 ingredients in a large bowl; let stand 15 minutes. Add watermelon and next 2 ingredients, and gently toss to coat. Serve immediately, or cover and chill up to 24 hours.

GRILLED FLANK STEAK WITH GUACAMOLE SAUCE

SERVES 8
HANDS-ON 20 min.
TOTAL 35 min.

Dried chipotle powder may be found on the spice aisle of your supermarket. If you serve the flank steak without the Guacamole Sauce, reduce the chipotle powder to 1 tsp. to tame the heat.

1   (2-lb.) flank steak, trimmed
2   tsp. dried chipotle powder
1½ tsp. table salt
2   tsp. minced fresh garlic
16 (8-inch) flour tortillas (optional)
     Guacamole Sauce

1. Sprinkle steak evenly with chipotle powder and salt; rub with garlic.

2. Light charcoal grill or preheat gas grill to 350° to 400° (**medium-high**). Grill steak, covered with grill lid, 8 to 10 minutes on each side or until desired degree of doneness. Cover loosely with aluminum foil, and let stand 5 minutes.

3. Cut steak diagonally across the grain into thin strips. Serve with tortillas, if desired, and Guacamole Sauce.

GUACAMOLE SAUCE

Makes: 1½ cups   Hands-on: 5 min.   Total: 6 min.

2   small ripe avocados, peeled   ½   tsp. grated lime zest
     and cut into quarters   ¼   cup fresh lime juice
1   small jalapeño pepper,   ½   tsp. table salt
     seeded and minced   ½   tsp. sugar
1   green onion, sliced   ¼   tsp. minced fresh garlic
½   cup fat-free sour cream

1. Process all ingredients in a blender or food processor 30 seconds or until smooth.

CILANTRO-GINGER FLANK STEAK WITH EDAMAME RICE

Frozen edamame comes two ways, shelled and unshelled. If you can only find unshelled, steam the pods first to easily remove the interior beans.

SERVES 4
HANDS-ON 30 min.
TOTAL 30 min.

1   Tbsp. grated fresh ginger
1   Tbsp. olive oil
6   Tbsp. chopped fresh cilantro, divided
1   (1-lb.) flank steak
1   tsp. table salt
½   tsp. freshly ground black pepper
½   lime
2   (8.5-oz.) pouches ready-to-serve basmati rice
2   cups fully cooked shelled frozen edamame, thawed

1. Light charcoal grill or preheat gas grill to 400° to 450° (**high**). Stir together ginger, oil, and 2 Tbsp. cilantro in a small bowl; rub mixture on steak. Sprinkle with salt and pepper.

2. Grill steak, covered with grill lid, 6 to 7 minutes on each side or until desired degree of doneness. Remove from grill; squeeze juice from lime over steak. Cover loosely with aluminum foil, and let stand 10 minutes.

3. Meanwhile, prepare rice according to package directions; stir in edamame and remaining 4 Tbsp. cilantro. Cut steak across the grain into thin slices; serve over rice mixture.

GRILLED FILET MIGNON WITH RED WINE MUSHROOM SAUCE

SERVES 4
HANDS-ON 35 min.
TOTAL 40 min.

Butter and a splash of heavy cream add richness to the sauce that's spooned over these tender filets.

⅓ cup butter, divided

2 Tbsp. finely chopped shallots

1 tsp. minced garlic

1 (8-oz.) container sliced baby portobello mushrooms

¾ cup dry red wine

¼ cup low-sodium fat-free beef broth

1 Tbsp. Worcestershire sauce

2 tsp. coarse-grained Dijon mustard

2 Tbsp. heavy cream

4 (8-oz.) beef tenderloin filets (1 inch thick)

1 Tbsp. olive oil

½ tsp. kosher salt

½ tsp. freshly ground black pepper

1. Light charcoal grill or preheat gas grill to 350° to 400° (**medium-high**). Melt 1½ Tbsp. butter in a medium saucepan over medium heat. Add shallots and garlic; sauté 2 minutes or until tender. Add mushrooms; sauté 3 minutes or until tender. Stir in wine, broth, Worcestershire sauce, and mustard. Cook 14 to 16 minutes or until liquid is reduced by half. Stir in cream; cook 1 minute. Add remaining butter, stirring until butter melts. Keep warm.

2. Rub steaks with oil, and sprinkle with salt and pepper. Grill, covered with lid, 8 minutes on each side or until desired degree of doneness. Remove from grill; let stand 5 minutes. Serve with sauce.

STEP-BY-STEP

1. If you have a gas grill with a side burner, make this rich topping in the great outdoors.

2. The sauce is so robust, the steaks only need salt and pepper for flavor.

ASIAN GRILLED TRI-TIP

This dish is my take on an old favorite from TenPenh, the now-closed Asian-inspired restaurant I helped open in Washington, D.C. The tri-tip would rest in a robust marinade with black Asian vinegar, sesame, and garlic, flavors that fused together to give the meat an ideal combination of tenderness and exceptionally complex flavors. Once the meat was placed on the grill, the kitchen would immediately be filled with a mouthwatering aroma that conjured visions of street vendors around the urban neighborhoods of Southeast Asia. The finished meat would get tossed into a wok with chow foon noodles, farmers' market vegetables, and a spicy hoisin sauce.

SERVES 4

HANDS-ON 20 min.

TOTAL 20 min., plus 8 hr. for marinating

1 (1½- to 2-lb.) beef tri-tip, cut into 2-inch cubes
¼ cup low-sodium soy sauce
¼ cup black Asian vinegar
½ cup peanut or vegetable oil
3 Tbsp. honey
4 green onions, thinly sliced
2 Tbsp. fresh ginger, peeled and minced
¼ cup chili garlic sauce
2 Tbsp. black and white sesame seeds
Additional black or white sesame seeds
Rice or rice noodles

1. Place a 1-gal. zip-top plastic freezer bag in a large bowl; add first 9 ingredients. Seal bag, and turn it to mix well; refrigerate 8 to 10 hours. About 1 hour before grilling beef, light charcoal grill or preheat gas grill to 400° to 500° (**high**).

2. Remove beef from marinade, discarding marinade, and grill 2 minutes; turn and grill an additional 2 minutes. Remove beef from grill, and sprinkle with additional sesame seeds. Serve over rice or rice noodles.

David's TIPS

High heat is key here because these pieces of steak don't take long to cook and can dry out pretty easily. Be sure to preheat the grill and get it really hot, then just sear the meat for a couple minutes to get a good char.

QUICK-MARINATED GRILLED BISON HANGER STEAKS

SERVES 4

HANDS-ON 8 min.

TOTAL 1 hr., 18 min.

Grilled bison is more tender than beef. Sometimes called "butcher's filet," this delicate meat can be special ordered where fresh meats are sold. You may, however, substitute beef hanger steak.

2   garlic cloves, minced

3   Tbsp. olive oil

½   tsp. dried crushed red pepper

4   (8-oz.) bison hanger steaks
    Kosher salt
    Freshly ground black pepper

1. Combine garlic, olive oil, and red pepper in a small bowl; mix well, and place into a 1-gal. zip-top plastic freezer bag. Add steaks; squeeze out air, and seal bag. Let steaks marinate at room temperature 1 hour. Meanwhile, light charcoal grill or preheat gas grill to 400° to 500° (**high**).

2. Remove steaks from marinade, discarding marinade. Place on cooking grate, and season with salt and black pepper; grill 4 minutes. Turn steaks, and season with salt and black pepper; grill 4 more minutes or until a meat thermometer inserted into thickest portion registers 130° to 135° (medium-rare to medium). Remove from grill, and let stand 8 to 10 minutes before slicing and serving.

BLUE CHEESE–TOPPED STRIP STEAKS

SERVES 4
HANDS-ON 22 min.
TOTAL 22 min.

Soft, fresh breadcrumbs and moist blue cheese crumbled straight from the block create a flavorful topping for the steaks.

½ cup crumbled blue cheese
¼ cup soft, fresh breadcrumbs
1 tsp. chopped fresh parsley
1 tsp. finely chopped shallots
3 garlic cloves, minced
4 (12-oz.) beef strip steaks (1½ inches thick)
2 Tbsp. olive oil
½ tsp. kosher salt
½ tsp. freshly ground black pepper

1. Light charcoal grill or preheat gas grill to 350° to 400° (**medium-high**). Toss together first 5 ingredients in a medium bowl. Rub steaks with oil, and sprinkle with salt and pepper.

2. Grill steaks, covered with grill lid, 3 minutes on each side. Remove steaks from grill; top with cheese mixture. Return steaks to grill, and grill, covered with grill lid, 3 more minutes or until desired degree of doneness and topping is browned.

GRILLED VEAL CHOPS WITH ARTICHOKES AND ARUGULA SALAD

SERVES 4
HANDS-ON 20 min.
TOTAL 1 hr., 24 min.

The intense peppery-mustard flavor of arugula works nicely with these simple grilled veal chops, creating a meal worthy of company with minimal effort.

4 (7-oz.) veal loin chops (about ½ inch thick)
¾ tsp. freshly ground black pepper, divided
½ tsp. table salt, divided
1½ Tbsp. olive oil, divided
1 tsp. grated fresh lemon zest
3 garlic cloves, minced
   Vegetable cooking spray
1 (5-oz.) package baby arugula or spinach
1 (14-oz.) can artichoke bottoms, drained and thinly sliced
¼ cup coarsely chopped walnuts, toasted
1 Tbsp. fresh lemon juice

1. Sprinkle veal chops evenly with ½ tsp. pepper and ¼ tsp. salt. Combine 1½ tsp. olive oil, lemon zest, and garlic; rub over veal chops. Cover and chill 1 to 4 hours.

2. Light charcoal grill or preheat gas grill to 350° to 400° (**medium-high**). Place veal chops on grill rack coated with cooking spray; grill 4 minutes on each side or until desired degree of doneness.

3. While veal cooks, combine arugula, artichokes, and walnuts in a bowl. Combine remaining ¼ tsp. each of pepper and salt, remaining 1 Tbsp. olive oil, and lemon juice; drizzle over salad, and toss well. Serve immediately with veal chops.

David's
TIPS

Prepare the veal chops up to four hours ahead, and grill them just before you're ready to eat.

SMOKED BEEF TENDERLOIN

1 (5-lb.) beef tenderloin, trimmed

Wood chips

2 Tbsp. olive oil

2 Tbsp. Hill Country Rub

Vegetable cooking spray

Chimichurri Sauce

SERVES 8 to 10
HANDS-ON 35 min.
TOTAL 2 hr., 29 min., plus 12 hr. for chilling

1. Let tenderloin stand, covered, at room temperature 1 hour. Meanwhile, soak wood chips in water 30 minutes. Prepare smoker according to manufacturer's directions, bringing internal temperature to 300°; maintain temperature for 15 to 20 minutes.

2. Pat tenderloin dry; brush with oil, and sprinkle with Hill Country Rub. Drain wood chips, and place on coals. Place tenderloin on cooking grate; cover with smoker lid. Smoke tenderloin, maintaining temperature inside smoker at 300°, for 45 minutes or until a meat thermometer inserted into thickest portion registers 130°. Let stand at room temperature 30 minutes; cover and chill 12 to 24 hours.

3. Coat cold cooking grate with cooking spray, and place on grill. Light charcoal grill or preheat gas grill to 400° to 500° (**high**). Place chilled tenderloin on cooking grate, and grill 2 minutes on each side. Let stand 5 minutes before slicing. Serve with Chimichurri Sauce.

HILL COUNTRY RUB

Makes: 1¾ cups   Hands-on: 5 min.   Total: 5 min.

1½ cups kosher salt

¼ cup coarsely ground black pepper

2 Tbsp. ground red pepper

1. Stir together all ingredients.

CHIMICHURRI SAUCE

Makes: 1½ cups   Hands-on: 5 min.   Total: 5 min.

4 cups firmly packed fresh flat-leaf parsley

¾ cup olive oil

4 garlic cloves

3 Tbsp. fresh lemon juice

3 Tbsp. red wine vinegar

2 Tbsp. minced shallot

1 tsp. kosher salt

½ tsp. freshly ground black pepper

½ tsp. dried crushed red pepper

1. Process all ingredients in a food processor until finely chopped.

STEAK AND FINGERLING POTATO KABOBS

SERVES 6

HANDS-ON 45 min.

TOTAL 1 hr., 20 min., plus 3 hr. for marinating

Parboiling fingerling potatoes jump-starts the cooking process, so they take on a crispy finish just about the time the steak is done.

14 (8-inch) wooden or metal skewers, divided

16 small fingerling potatoes, halved

2 lb. boneless rib-eye, tri-tip, or flank steaks, trimmed and cut into 1½-inch pieces

Béarnaise Vinaigrette, divided

¼ cup butter, melted

1 cup firmly packed baby arugula

1 cup loosely packed fresh flat-leaf parsley leaves

½ cup torn fresh basil

¼ cup chopped fresh chives

¼ cup loosely packed fresh mint leaves, torn

3 tsp. drained capers

1. Soak 8 wooden skewers in water 30 minutes (omit if using metal skewers).

2. Meanwhile, bring potatoes and water to cover to a boil in a Dutch oven over medium-high heat; cook 10 minutes or just until crisp-tender. Drain.

3. Combine steak and ½ cup vinaigrette in a large zip-top plastic freezer bag. Thread 8 potato halves onto 1 double set of skewers (2 skewers side by side), leaving ⅛-inch space between pieces; repeat with 3 double sets of skewers and remaining potatoes. Cut 4 to 8 crosswise slits ¼ inch deep on top of each potato. Combine potatoes and ½ cup vinaigrette in another large zip-top plastic freezer bag. Seal bags, and chill 3 hours, turning occasionally.

4. Meanwhile, soak remaining 6 wooden skewers in water 30 minutes (omit if using metal skewers).

5. Light charcoal grill or preheat gas grill to 350° to 400° (**medium-high**). Remove steak and potatoes from marinades; discard marinades. Thread steak onto 6 skewers, leaving ⅛-inch space between pieces. Sprinkle with desired amount of salt and pepper. Grill potatoes and steak at the same time, covered with grill lid, 6 to 7 minutes on each side or until desired degree of doneness and potatoes are golden brown, basting potatoes and steak with melted butter with each turn.

6. Toss together arugula, next 5 ingredients, and 2 Tbsp. vinaigrette. Serve kabobs with arugula salad and remaining vinaigrette.

BÉARNAISE VINAIGRETTE

Makes: about 2 cups   Hands-on: 5 min.   Total: 5 min.

¾ cup white wine vinegar

¼ cup chopped fresh tarragon

¼ cup fresh lemon juice

3 shallots, minced

2 garlic cloves, minced

1 Tbsp. Dijon mustard

2 tsp. sugar

1½ tsp. table salt

1 tsp. freshly ground black pepper

½ cup canola oil

½ cup olive oil

1. Whisk together vinegar and next 8 ingredients in a bowl. Add canola oil and olive oil, 1 at a time in a slow, steady stream, whisking constantly until mixture is smooth.

VIETNAMESE BBQ TACOS

STEP-BY-STEP

1. Marinating overnight ensures tender and flavorful steaks.

2. Grill directly over the fire, but leave an area to move the steaks if flare-ups occur.

3. Before slicing, let the meat stand 10 minutes for the juices to reabsorb.

For a fun party meal, grill the tortillas alongside the steak and set out a topping bar for your guests to custom build this delicious street food.

¼ cup fish sauce	3 beef strip steaks (about 2½ lb.)
¼ cup rice wine vinegar	8 (8-inch) soft taco-size flour tortillas, warmed
2 Tbsp. grated fresh ginger	Vietnamese Dipping Sauce
3 garlic cloves, minced	Toppings: thinly sliced red cabbage, matchstick carrots, thinly sliced red onion, chopped fresh cilantro, chopped fresh mint, cucumber slices
2 Tbsp. sugar	
2 Tbsp. honey	
1 Tbsp. sesame oil	
1 tsp. freshly ground black pepper	
½ medium-size red onion, sliced	

1. Whisk together fish sauce and next 7 ingredients in a large shallow dish or zip-top plastic freezer bag; stir in red onion slices, and add steaks, turning to coat. Cover or seal, and chill 8 to 24 hours, turning once.

2. Light charcoal grill or preheat gas grill to 350° to 400° (**medium-high**). Remove steaks from marinade; discard marinade. Grill steaks 7 to 8 minutes on each side or until desired degree of doneness, turning every 3 to 5 minutes; remove from grill.

3. Cover steaks loosely with aluminum foil, and let stand 10 minutes. Cut steaks across the grain into thin strips, and serve in warm flour tortillas with Vietnamese Dipping Sauce and desired toppings

VIETNAMESE DIPPING SAUCE

Makes: 1 cup Hands-on: 5 min. Total: 5 min.

¼ cup fish sauce	2 garlic cloves, minced
¼ cup white vinegar	1 serrano pepper or Thai chile pepper, seeded and sliced
3 Tbsp. sugar	
2 Tbsp. fresh lime juice	

1. Stir together ½ cup water, fish sauce, and remaining ingredients in a medium bowl. Refrigerate in an airtight container up to 1 week.

BEER-AND-BROWN SUGAR RIB-EYE STEAKS

SERVES 4

HANDS-ON 12 min.

TOTAL 17 min., plus
1 day for marinating

Your favorite dark beer, teriyaki sauce, and brown sugar combine to create a simple yet flavorful marinade for juicy rib-eye steaks.

½ cup dark beer

¼ cup teriyaki marinade and sauce

¼ cup firmly packed brown sugar

4 (1-inch-thick) rib-eye steaks (about 3 lb.)

¾ tsp. kosher salt

¾ tsp. freshly ground black pepper

1. Whisk together first 3 ingredients in a large shallow dish or zip-top plastic freezer bag; add steaks, turning to coat. Cover or seal, and chill 24 hours, turning once.

2. Light charcoal grill or preheat gas grill to 350° to 400° (**medium-high**). Remove steaks from marinade; discard marinade. Sprinkle steaks with salt and pepper. Grill steaks, covered with grill lid, 5 minutes on each side or until desired degree of doneness. Remove steaks from grill, and let stand 5 minutes before serving.

PRIME CHOICE

Rib-eye steaks come from the rib section of the cow. Look for steaks that have nice marbling (lines of fat running through the meat), and trim off any thicker areas of fat before marinating.

GRILLED STEAKS BALSAMICO

For a bolder sweet, salty flavor, serve the steaks with the cheese sauce and pass around extra fig preserves.

SERVES 4

HANDS-ON 15 min.

TOTAL 18 min., plus 2 hr. for marinating

⅔ cup balsamic vinaigrette

¼ cup fig preserves

4 (6- to 8-oz.) boneless beef chuck-eye steaks

1 tsp. table salt

1 tsp. freshly ground black pepper

1 (6.5-oz.) container buttery garlic-and-herb spreadable cheese

1. Process vinaigrette and preserves in a blender until smooth. Place steaks and vinaigrette mixture in a shallow dish or a large zip-top plastic freezer bag. Cover or seal, and chill at least 2 hours. Remove steaks from marinade, discarding marinade.

2. Light charcoal grill or preheat gas grill to 350° to 400° (**medium-high**). Grill, covered with grill lid, 5 to 7 minutes on each side or until desired degree of doneness. Remove to a serving platter, and sprinkle evenly with salt and pepper; keep warm.

3. Heat cheese in a small saucepan over low heat, stirring often, 2 to 4 minutes or until melted. Serve cheese sauce with steaks.

BEEF RIBS WITH SORGHUM GLAZE

SERVES 8

HANDS-ON 45 min.

TOTAL 6 hr., 25 min., plus 12 hr. for marinating

Sorghum syrup is similar in taste and viscosity to blackstrap molasses.

4   (2½-lb.) racks beef rib-back ribs (center cut)
¼   cup sugar
¼   cup kosher salt
2   Tbsp. freshly ground black pepper
1   tsp. garlic powder
1   tsp. onion powder
1   tsp. smoked paprika
½   tsp. ground red pepper
1   cup sorghum syrup
1   cup cider vinegar
1   Tbsp. coarsely ground black pepper
4   cups wood chips

1. Rinse and pat ribs dry. Remove thin membrane from back of ribs by slicing into it and pulling it off. Combine sugar and next 6 ingredients. Massage sugar mixture into meat, covering all sides. Wrap ribs tightly with plastic wrap, and place in zip-top plastic freezer bags; seal and chill 12 hours.

2. Whisk together sorghum and next 2 ingredients in a saucepan over medium-high heat. Bring to a boil, stirring occasionally; reduce heat to medium, and cook, stirring occasionally, 6 minutes or until mixture is reduced by half. Cool completely.

3. Soak chips in water 30 minutes. Light 1 side of charcoal grill or preheat gas grill to 250° to 300° (**medium-low**); leave other side unlit. Spread wood chips on a large sheet of heavy-duty aluminum foil; fold edges to seal. Poke several holes in top of pouch with a fork. Place pouch directly on lit side of grill; cover with grill lid.

4. Place ribs over unlit side, and grill, covered with grill lid, 2 hours. Turn rib slabs over; grill 2 hours or until tender. Cook ribs 30 more minutes, basting frequently with sorghum mixture.

5. Remove ribs from grill, and let stand 10 minutes. Cut ribs, slicing between bones.

TEXAS SMOKED BRISKET

Wood chips
½ cup Brisket Dry Rub

1 (6½-lb.) flat-cut brisket
Brisket Red Sauce

SERVES 12 to 14
HANDS-ON 20 min.
TOTAL 6 hr., 40 min.

1. Soak wood chips in water 30 minutes. Prepare smoker according to manufacturer's directions, bringing internal temperature to 225° to 250°; maintain temperature for 15 to 20 minutes. Sprinkle Brisket Dry Rub on brisket, patting to adhere. Let stand 10 minutes. Drain wood chips; place on the coals. Place brisket on upper rack; cover with lid.

2. Smoke brisket, maintaining temperature inside smoker between 225° to 250°, for 5½ to 6 hours or until a meat thermometer inserted into thickest portion registers between 195° to 205°. Add additional charcoal and wood chips as needed. Remove brisket from smoker, and cut across grain into thin slices; serve with Brisket Red Sauce.

BRISKET DRY RUB

Makes: 2 cups   Hands-on: 10 min.   Total: 10 min.

¾ cup paprika
¼ cup kosher salt
¼ cup sugar
¼ cup freshly ground black pepper
2 Tbsp. chili powder

2 Tbsp. onion powder
2 Tbsp. ground chipotle chile pepper
2 Tbsp. ancho chile powder
1½ Tbsp. garlic powder
2 tsp. ground red pepper

1. Stir together all ingredients. Store in an airtight container in a cool, dark place up to 6 months.

BRISKET RED SAUCE

Makes: 3¼ cups   Hands-on: 10 min.   Total: 10 min.

1½ cups cider vinegar
1 cup ketchup
¼ cup firmly packed light brown sugar
¼ cup Worcestershire sauce
2 Tbsp. unsalted butter
1½ tsp. onion powder

1½ tsp. granulated garlic
1½ tsp. ground cumin
1 tsp. kosher salt
½ tsp. freshly ground black pepper
½ tsp. ground red pepper

1. Whisk together all ingredients in a saucepan. Bring to a boil over high heat; stir until butter melts. Remove from heat; serve warm.

GRILLED VENISON SAUSAGE WITH MUSTARD DIPPING SAUCE

MAKES about 30 patties
HANDS-ON 12 min.
TOTAL 22 min.

Deer hunting is my passion in the fall and winter, so in January I always have a freezer full of venison. Making sausage is a great way to use up the less desirable cuts. Because it's a wild animal, the meat is lean and gamey, so I always add fat to keep the sausage moist. (If you're buying ground meat from the butcher, be sure to ask for some fatback as well.)

3 lb. trimmed venison, cut into 1-inch pieces
1 lb. fatback, cut into 1-inch pieces
¼ tsp. ground cloves
2 Tbsp. caraway seeds, toasted
1 Tbsp. dried crushed red pepper
1 Tbsp. Spanish paprika
2 Tbsp. kosher salt
2 Tbsp. freshly ground black pepper
1 Tbsp. ground sage
½ cup ice water
Mustard Dipping Sauce

1. Grind venison and fatback using the medium plate of a meat grinder. Set aside.

2. Stir together next 7 ingredients and ½ cup ice water; pour into meat mixture, and mix thoroughly for at least 2 minutes.

3. Light charcoal grill or preheat gas grill to 350° (**medium**). Dip hands in water, and shape meat mixture into 2-oz. patties. Grill, uncovered, for 8 to 10 minutes. Serve with Mustard Dipping Sauce.

MUSTARD DIPPING SAUCE

Makes: 3 cups   Hands-on: 5 min.   Total: 5 min.

1 cup dry mustard
1 cup water
⅔ cup white vinegar
2 tsp. all-purpose flour
1 Tbsp. kosher salt
½ tsp. turmeric
½ tsp. garlic powder

1. Whisk together all ingredients in a small saucepan until smooth. Bring to a boil over medium-high heat, and cook, stirring occasionally, 7 to 8 minutes. Cool 5 minutes before serving. Refrigerate in an airtight container up to 1 month.

David's
TIPS

You can grind the meat for these sausage patties ahead of time and refrigerate it in an airtight container up to 3 days or freeze up to 1 month.

GRILLED LAMB NECK WITH MINT CHIMICHURRI

My time hosting Travel Channel's *American Grilled* was eye-opening for me as a chef. I learned so much from the contestants and farmers I met along the way. We filmed the final episode at Jamison Farm in Latrobe, Pennsylvania—home of Arnold Palmer, Rolling Rock, and Mister Rogers. John Jamison and his wife, Sukey, raise more than 5,000 lambs annually, which are provided to notable chefs worldwide. I was able to witness firsthand how remarkably talented they are as butchers. They told me a best-kept secret that prominent chefs are putting lamb necks on their menus. In this recipe, the addition of Mint Chimichurri brightens up the richly saturated meatiness of the lamb.

SERVES 4
HANDS-ON 10 min.
TOTAL 17 min.

4   lamb neck fillets
    Kosher salt

Freshly ground black pepper
Mint Chimichurri

1. Light charcoal grill or preheat gas grill to 350° to 400° (**medium-high**). Season fillets with salt and pepper, and place on cooking grate. Grill 5 minutes; turn and grill an additional 5 minutes or until a meat thermometer inserted into thickest portion registers 130° (medium-rare). Remove fillets from grill, and let stand 5 to 7 minutes. Serve with Mint Chimichurri.

MINT CHIMICHURRI

Makes: 1 cup   Hands-on: 5 min.   Total: 5 min.

1   cup firmly packed fresh mint leaves
½   cup firmly packed flat-leaf parsley
2   garlic cloves, chopped
1   tsp. dried crushed red pepper
½   cup olive oil
⅓   cup red wine vinegar

1. Place all ingredients in bowl of a food processor; pulse 15 to 20 times or until well blended but not overly pureed. Cover and set aside until ready to use, or refrigerate in an airtight container up to 1 week.

PRIME CHOICE

Plain organic yogurt offers the perfect tangy acidity to this dish. Just spoon some into a bowl and top it with a drizzle of good extra virgin olive oil and a sprinkle of Maldon sea salt, or any other flakey finishing salt.

FISH AND SHELLFISH

FISHING IS A WAY OF LIFE IN LOUISIANA—even the license plates read "Sportsman's Paradise." My hometown of New Orleans is close to where the waters of The Gulf kiss the Mississippi River, producing one of the most fabled sport-fishing grounds. Thanks to this natural wonder, Louisiana is home to more than 40% of the nation's coastal wetlands, containing some of the world's most diverse seafood habitats.

I grew up along a subdivision lake, where the waters were calmer and not as bountiful. As kids, two others from the neighborhood and I were practically the only ones to fish on that lake. I would squeeze a piece of white bread onto my hook—forbidden for eating, but permissible as fish bait—and cast my line out into the water to snag a perch. There is something wonderfully honest, even morally exemplary about catching your own fish. I'd come home with a bucket full, much to my mother's dismay, but I was always so proud of my catch that she'd clean and fry them whole with the heads on.

As I got older, I took my backyard hobby to the open air and open waters of the Gulf. I found that the activity still remained simple, and the glory of the catch was exhilarating. The excitement heightened when the line started zipping out and the game of reeling and pumping began. Then there it was—the silvery, glistening fish at the end of the tightened line.

It is captivating to see a discerning cook like my dad prepare fish, with each piece geometrically marked by the grate in an attractive pattern. It is a sight that makes one appreciate the natural ability of the heat of the coals and wood chips. You'll be "hooked" on this chapter with some new, interesting techniques for cooking fish with unique sauces and rubs.

Brown Bag-Wrapped
Whole Fish, page 221

SWEET ASIAN GRILLED SALMON

Brown sugar and hot mustard come together with soy sauce to make a "sweet-hot" glaze.

Vegetable cooking spray

¼ cup Chinese hot mustard

3 Tbsp. dark brown sugar

1 Tbsp. soy sauce

1 tsp. rice vinegar

6 (6-oz.) skinless salmon fillets (1¼ inches thick)

SERVES 6

HANDS-ON 8 min.

TOTAL 14 min.

1. Coat cold cooking grate with cooking spray, and place on grill. Light charcoal grill or preheat gas grill to 350° to 400° (**medium-high**). Whisk together mustard and next 3 ingredients in a bowl; reserve ⅓ cup mustard mixture to serve with cooked fillets. Brush half of remaining mustard mixture over 1 side of fillets.

2. Place fillets, mustard sides down, on cooking grate. Grill, covered with grill lid, 4 minutes. Turn fillets over, and brush with remaining half of mustard mixture; grill, covered with grill lid, 2 minutes or just until fish flakes with a fork. Serve fillets with reserved mustard mixture.

STEP-BY-STEP

1. Place salmon flesh side down to get a nice sear.

2. Flip the fillets to crisp the skin and continue to brush with the mustard glaze.

GRILLED SEA BASS WITH MANGO SALSA

SERVES 4

HANDS-ON 14 min.

TOTAL 14 min.

Choose fish fillets that are even in size and shape. They should be about 1¼ inch thick. There's no shortage of salsa with this recipe, so pile it high on each fish fillet. It's as colorful and refreshing as summertime itself.

2   cups chopped mango
1   cup chopped red bell pepper
⅔   cup chopped green onions
¼   cup chopped fresh cilantro
2   Tbsp. fresh lime juice
1½   tsp. kosher salt, divided
1½   tsp. freshly ground black pepper, divided
4   (6-oz.) sea bass fillets

1. Toss together mango, next 4 ingredients, ½ tsp. salt, and ½ tsp. pepper in a medium bowl; set aside.

2. Light charcoal grill or preheat gas grill to 350° to 400° (**medium-high**). Sprinkle fillets with remaining 1 tsp. salt and remaining 1 tsp. pepper. Grill fillets, covered with grill lid, 3 minutes on each side or just until fish flakes with a fork. Serve with mango salsa.

STEP-BY-STEP

1. Make the salsa ahead of time so that the flavors meld while grilling the fish.

2. Liberally sprinkle fillets with salt and pepper.

3. Don't move the fish until it comes up easily from the grill grate.

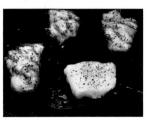

TERIYAKI-GLAZED GRILLED SALMON

SERVES 4
HANDS-ON 37 min.
TOTAL 1 hr., 7 min.

Jasmine rice and broccoli make ideal sides for these fillets, which are seasoned with citrus juices, teriyaki sauce, and fresh ginger.

Citrus-Teriyaki Glaze, divided

Vegetable cooking spray

4 (6-oz.) salmon fillets

2 Tbsp. olive oil

1 tsp. kosher salt

1 tsp. coarsely ground black pepper

1. Prepare Citrus-Teriyaki Glaze. Reserve ¼ cup glaze to serve with grilled salmon.

2. Coat cold cooking grate with cooking spray, and place on grill. Light charcoal grill or preheat gas grill to 350° to 400° (**medium-high**). Rub fillets with oil, and sprinkle with salt and pepper.

3. Place fillets, skin sides up, on cooking grate, and grill, covered with grill lid, 4 minutes. Turn fillets over; grill, covered with grill lid, 4 more minutes or just until fish flakes with a fork, basting often with remaining ½ cup glaze. Serve with reserved ¼ cup glaze.

CITRUS-TERIYAKI GLAZE

Makes: ¾ cup   Hands-on: 27 min.   Total: 57 min.

½ cup fresh orange juice

½ cup teriyaki sauce

¼ cup finely chopped green onions

3 Tbsp. fresh lime juice

2 Tbsp. minced fresh ginger

2 garlic cloves, minced

1. Stir together all ingredients in a small saucepan. Bring to a boil over medium-high heat, stirring often. Boil 10 minutes or until liquid is reduced by half. Remove from heat, and cool completely (about 30 minutes).

FIRECRACKER GRILLED SALMON

Salmon sticks easily to the grill. Be sure to oil the grill grates before placing the salmon.

½ cup vegetable oil

¼ cup reduced-sodium soy sauce

¼ cup balsamic vinegar

1 Tbsp. honey

2 tsp. finely chopped garlic

2 tsp. dried crushed red pepper

1½ tsp. ground ginger

1 tsp. sesame oil

½ tsp. table salt

¼ tsp. onion powder

6 (6-oz.) salmon fillets

SERVES 6
HANDS-ON 25 min.
TOTAL 55 min.

1. Whisk together first 10 ingredients in a large shallow dish or zip-top plastic freezer bag; reserve ¼ cup mixture for basting fillets. Add fillets to dish or bag; cover or seal, and chill 30 minutes.

2. Light charcoal grill or preheat gas grill to 400° to 500° **(high)**. Remove fillets from marinade; discard marinade. Grill fillets, without grill lid, 4 to 5 minutes or just until fish flakes with a fork, turning occasionally and basting with reserved ¼ cup marinade. Remove from grill, and discard skin before serving.

GRILLED REDFISH AND CORN MAQUE CHOUX WITH BEURRE BLANC

SERVES 6
HANDS-ON 11 min.
TOTAL 11 min.

Redfish is a common name for many types of fish, such as red snapper or ocean perch. Grilling ears of corn in the husks before slicing off the kernels gives this dish a smoky-sweet taste.

6	(8-oz.) redfish fillets, skin and scales on
¼	cup olive oil
	Table salt

Freshly ground black pepper
Grilled Corn Maque Choux
Beurre Blanc

1. Light charcoal grill or preheat gas grill to 350° to 400° (**medium-high**). Brush fillets with oil, and season with salt and pepper. Place fillets, flesh sides down, on cooking grate, and grill 2 to 3 minutes. Turn fillets, and place, scale sides down, on cooking grate; cook an additional 6 to 8 minutes or until fish flakes with a fork. Remove fillets from grill.

2. Place Grilled Corn Maque Choux on each serving plate, and top with 1 fillet and Beurre Blanc.

GRILLED CORN MAQUE CHOUX

Makes: 3 cups Hands-on: 29 min. Total: 29 min.

4	ears fresh corn with husks	2	Tbsp. diced tomato
1	Tbsp. canola oil	2	tsp. diced green onions
1	Tbsp. butter	¾	cup heavy cream
2	Tbsp. diced onion		Table salt
1	Tbsp. diced celery		Freshly ground black pepper
1	Tbsp. diced red bell pepper		Ground red pepper
1	tsp. minced garlic	2	pickled okra pods, each sliced into 6 pieces

1. Light charcoal grill or preheat gas grill to 350° to 400° (**medium-high**). Rub corn husks with canola oil. Place corn on cooking grate, and grill 2 minutes; turn and repeat until all sides of the corn have deep color. Cool corn; remove husks, and cut kernels from cobs using a serrated knife. Discard cobs.

2. Melt butter in a sauté pan over medium-high heat. Add grilled corn kernels, onion, celery, red bell pepper, and garlic, and sauté 7 to 8 minutes or until translucent. Add tomato, green onions, and cream; cook

over medium-high heat 15 minutes or until cream is slightly reduced. Season with salt, black pepper, and red pepper. Stir in sliced okra, and remove from heat.

BEURRE BLANC

Makes: 2 cups   Hands-on: 10 min.   Total: 10 min.

1	cup white wine
½	lemon, thinly sliced
1	Tbsp. whole peppercorns
2	Tbsp. chopped shallots

1	lb. unsalted butter, cut into ½-inch pieces
½	tsp. kosher salt

1. Combine wine, lemon slices, peppercorns, and shallots in a saucepan over medium-high heat; simmer 5 minutes or until reduced by one-third. Add butter, one piece at a time, whisking vigorously. Remove from heat, and pour sauce through a fine wire-mesh strainer; discard solids. Season with salt. Cover sauce to keep warm.

TROPICAL GRILLED TUNA STEAKS

SERVES 4
HANDS-ON 12 min.
TOTAL 1 hr., 17 min.

Tuna is best served medium-rare, but if you prefer it medium or well done, add additional cook time.

1   cup pineapple juice
¼   cup hoisin sauce
2   Tbsp. fresh lime juice
1   Tbsp. chopped fresh cilantro
1   tsp. grated fresh ginger
1   tsp. dark sesame oil
4   (12-oz.) tuna steaks (1 inch thick)

1. Whisk together first 6 ingredients in a small bowl. Place ¾ cup juice mixture in a large shallow dish or zip-top plastic freezer bag; add steaks, turning to coat. Cover or seal, and chill 1 hour, turning once.

2. Light charcoal grill or preheat gas grill to 400° to 500° (**high**). Remove steaks from marinade; discard marinade.

3. Grill steaks, covered with grill lid, 2 minutes on each side or just until fish flakes with a fork.

4. Meanwhile, bring remaining ¾ cup juice mixture to a boil in a small saucepan over medium-high heat, and boil 5 minutes or until reduced to ½ cup. Serve with grilled steaks.

POBLANO FISH TACOS

Top with crumbled queso fresco and grill the corn tortillas for a tasty variation.

SERVES 6
HANDS-ON 22 min.
TOTAL 42 min.

1   large poblano pepper
½   English cucumber, coarsely chopped
1   cup grape tomatoes, quartered
2   Tbsp. chopped red onion
1   garlic clove, minced
½   tsp. table salt
3   Tbsp. fresh lime juice, divided
4   Tbsp. olive oil, divided
1   Tbsp. mango-lime seafood seasoning
1½   lb. grouper or other firm-textured white fish fillets
12   (6-inch) fajita-size corn tortillas, warmed
     Lime wedges

1. Light charcoal grill or preheat gas grill to 350° to 400° (**medium-high**). Grill pepper, covered with grill lid, 3 to 4 minutes or until pepper looks blistered, turning once. Place pepper in a zip-top plastic freezer bag; seal and let stand 10 minutes to loosen skin. Peel pepper; remove and discard seeds. Coarsely chop.

2. Combine pepper, cucumber, next 4 ingredients, 2 Tbsp. lime juice, and 2 Tbsp. oil in a bowl.

3. Whisk together seafood seasoning, remaining 1 Tbsp. lime juice, and remaining 2 Tbsp. oil in a large shallow dish or zip-top plastic freezer bag; add fillets, turning to coat. Cover or seal, and chill 5 minutes, turning once. Remove fillets from marinade; discard marinade.

4. Grill fillets, covered with grill lid, 3 to 4 minutes on each side or just until fish flakes with a fork. Cool 5 minutes; flake into bite-size pieces. Serve with salsa in warm tortillas with lime wedges.

PRIME CHOICE

If you can't find grouper, choose another firm-textured fish such as halibut, mahi-mahi or tuna.

BLACKENED GRILLED CATFISH FILLETS

SERVES 6
HANDS-ON 12 min.
TOTAL 12 min.

Heavily coated with spices, these fillets pair well with a cool summer slaw.

2   Tbsp. kosher salt
3   Tbsp. paprika
1   tsp. granulated garlic
1   tsp. ground red pepper
½   tsp. dried oregano
½   tsp. dried thyme
½   tsp. freshly ground black pepper
½   tsp. ancho chile pepper
6   farm-raised catfish fillets
2   Tbsp. olive oil
    Garnish: lemon wedges

1. Light charcoal grill or preheat gas grill to 350° to 400° (**medium-high**). Stir together first 8 ingredients in a small bowl. Rub fillets with oil, and sprinkle with spice mixture (this should form a paste).

2. Grill fillets, covered with grill lid, 4 minutes on each side or just until fish flakes with a fork.

GRILLED TRIGGERFISH

SERVES 4

HANDS-ON 10 min.

TOTAL 10 min.

Freshness counts with a recipe this elemental. Meaty, just-caught triggerfish, or any other fresh, firm-textured fillets, will work—just adjust the grilling time depending on the thickness of the fish.

Vegetable cooking spray

4   (6-oz.) triggerfish, amberjack, cobia, mahi-mahi, swordfish, mackerel, or salmon fillets

2   Tbsp. extra virgin olive oil

½   tsp. table salt

¼   tsp. freshly ground black pepper

4   lemon wedges or 1 tsp. lemon zest (optional)

1. Coat cold cooking grate with cooking spray, and place on grill. Light charcoal grill or preheat gas grill to 350° to 400° (**medium-high**).

2. Brush both sides of fillets with oil; sprinkle with salt and pepper. Grill fillets, covered with grill lid, 4 minutes or until grill marks appear and fillets no longer stick to grate.

3. Using a metal spatula, carefully turn fillets over, and grill, without grill lid, 2 minutes or just until fish flakes with a fork. Serve with lemon wedges, or sprinkle with zest, if desired.

BROWN BAG—WRAPPED WHOLE FISH

This is a great way to recycle paper bags from grocery shopping. This technique uses a bag, soaked in water, to create a pouch to steam the fish. The paper bag packets go directly on the coals with the grill lid down. The result is a fantastically moist fish shot through with a touch of smokiness.

MAKES 2 whole fish
HANDS-ON 35 min.
TOTAL 1 hr., 25 min.

- 2 large brown-paper grocery bags, soaked in water 20 minutes
- 2 (14- x 24-inch) pieces aluminum foil
- 2 (1- to 1½-lb.) whole Chesapeake rockfish or other striped bass, cleaned and scaled
- 4 Tbsp. extra virgin olive oil
- 2 lemons
- 2 oz. ground thyme
- 3 shallots, thinly sliced
- 1 Tbsp. kosher salt
- ½ tsp. freshly ground black pepper

1. Light charcoal grill, banking coals along sides of grill and leaving center space open. Let coals burn 30 minutes or until smoldering before grilling fish. Cut open bags, and place flat on work surface; place 1 piece of aluminum foil on each bag.

2. Rinse fish under cold water, and pat dry with paper towels. Trim tail fins to make sure fish are no longer than 13 inches. Make 3 small, shallow, diagonal cuts on both sides of each fish.

3. Drizzle 1 Tbsp. oil on each piece of foil, and top with 1 fish. Slice 1 lemon; stuff belly of each fish evenly with lemon slices, thyme, and shallots. Season outside of both sides of each fish evenly with salt and pepper, and drizzle with 1 Tbsp. of remaining oil. Cut remaining lemon in half, and squeeze juice evenly on top of both fish. Starting with a long side of foil, wrap each fish; turn wrapped fish upside down to help keep foil closed. Starting with a long side of brown paper, wrap each foil-covered fish; tuck in ends of short sides to seal. Immerse wrapped fish in water 1 minute or until paper is completely soaked.

4. Place wrapped fish in middle of lit coals; top wrapped fish with coals. Close grill lid, and grill fish 30 minutes (some of the paper may burn). Use a spatula to remove fish from coals, and place on flat surface. Gently unwrap fish, spraying any burning paper with water. Peel back foil; remove fish, and place on serving platter, pouring any juices in foil over fish.

David's TIPS

To make the fish on a gas grill, preheat grill to 300° to 350° (medium) leaving 1 side unlit. Continue with recipe, but carefully rotate wrapped fish halfway through grilling.

GRILLED GROUPER WITH CUCUMBER-WATERMELON SALSA

If you can't find grouper, substitute striped bass or mahi-mahi.

SERVES 4
HANDS-ON 21 min.
TOTAL 21 min.

4   (4-oz.) grouper fillets
1   tsp. freshly ground black pepper
1   tsp. table salt, divided
3   Tbsp. olive oil, divided
2   cups chopped seedless watermelon
¼   cup chopped pitted kalamata olives
½   English cucumber, chopped
1   small jalapeño pepper, seeded and minced
2   Tbsp. minced red onion
2   Tbsp. white balsamic vinegar

1. Light charcoal grill or preheat gas grill to 350° to 400° (**medium-high**). Sprinkle fillets with black pepper and ½ tsp. salt. Drizzle with 2 Tbsp. oil.

2. Grill fillets, covered with grill lid, 3 to 4 minutes on each side or just until fish flakes with a fork.

3. Meanwhile, combine chopped watermelon, next 5 ingredients, remaining ½ tsp. salt, and remaining 1 Tbsp. oil. Serve with grilled fillets.

CUMIN-DUSTED CATFISH SANDWICHES

SERVES 4
HANDS-ON 10 min.
TOTAL 18 min.

In New Orleans, catfish is everywhere you look, fried or blackened and tossed with Cajun seasoning. There's nothing quite like the way the soft, flakey fish melts in your mouth in an explosion of spicy flavor with delicate undertones of smokiness from the grill.

1   cup mayonnaise
3   Tbsp. orange juice
1   to 2 tsp. minced canned chipotle chiles in adobo sauce
1½ tsp. table salt, divided
¼   cup self-rising cornmeal
2   tsp. ground cumin
4   (6-oz.) catfish fillets
    Vegetable cooking spray
4   whole wheat buns, split and toasted
    Tomato slices
    Shredded lettuce

1. Light charcoal grill or preheat gas grill to 350° to 400° (**medium-high**). Stir together first 3 ingredients and ½ tsp. salt; set aside.

2. Combine cornmeal, cumin, and remaining 1 tsp. salt. Rinse fillets, and dredge in cornmeal mixture; spray evenly with cooking spray.

3. Grill fillets, covered with grill lid, 3 to 4 minutes on each side or just until fish flakes with a fork. Serve on buns with mayonnaise mixture, tomato slices, and shredded lettuce.

GRILLED SALMON KABOBS

If you think cucumbers are best saved for gazpacho and tea sandwiches, you're in for a delicious surprise when you try this spice-crusted salmon teamed up with smoky, crunchy grilled cukes. A creamy yogurt raita, spiked with fresh dill and tangy bits of pickled okra, cools it all down.

SERVES 6
HANDS-ON 30 min.
TOTAL 30 min., plus 3 hr. for marinating

3   tsp. ground coriander
2   tsp. ground cumin
1   tsp. table salt
½   tsp. ground red pepper
1   (2¼-lb.) whole skinless salmon fillet, cut into 1-inch cubes
1   cup plain yogurt
⅓   cup finely chopped pickled okra
1   Tbsp. olive oil
2   tsp. chopped fresh dill
1½ tsp. fresh lemon juice
6   (12-inch) wooden or metal skewers
3   Kirby cucumbers
12 grape tomatoes
    Garnish: chopped fresh dill

1. Stir together first 4 ingredients in a large shallow bowl or large zip-top plastic freezer bag; add salmon. Cover or seal, and turn gently to coat. Chill 3 hours, turning occasionally.

2. Meanwhile, stir together yogurt and next 4 ingredients; cover and chill until ready to serve. Soak wooden skewers in water 30 minutes (omit if using metal skewers).

3. Light charcoal grill or preheat gas grill to 350° to 400° (**medium-high**). Scrape outside of cucumbers lengthwise using tines of a fork, scoring skin all the way around; cut into half moons.

4. Remove salmon from marinade; discard marinade. Thread salmon, cucumbers, and tomatoes alternately onto skewers, leaving ⅛-inch space between pieces. Grill kabobs, covered with grill lid, 5 to 6 minutes on each side or until desired degree of doneness. Serve with yogurt mixture.

FISH KABOBS

SERVES 2 to 3
HANDS-ON 24 min.
TOTAL 54 min.

Soaking the skewers in water prevents them from catching fire during grilling. If you have metal skewers, use those instead.

6   (6-inch) wooden skewers
1   (8-oz.) tuna fillet
1   (8-oz.) grouper fillet
1   (8-oz.) salmon fillet, skinned
1   (8-oz.) bottle olive oil-and-vinegar dressing
¼   cup chopped fresh flat-leaf parsley
1   Tbsp. fresh rosemary, chopped
1   Tbsp. pink peppercorns
2   Tbsp. fresh lemon juice
    Fresh herb sprigs (optional)

1. Soak skewers in water 30 minutes. Cut each fillet into 1-inch pieces, and thread onto skewers. Place kabobs in a shallow dish.

2. Stir together dressing and next 4 ingredients. Pour over kabobs; add fresh herb sprigs, if desired. Cover and chill 30 minutes.

3. Preheat grill to 400° to 500° (**high**). Remove kabobs from marinade; discard marinade. Grill kabobs, covered with grill lid, 4 minutes on each side or until desired degree of doneness.

STEP-BY-STEP

1. When skewering, alternate cubed tuna, grouper, and salmon.

2. Marinating for 30 minutes is plenty of time to add flavor to the fish.

3. Liberally oil the grill grates and place the skewers perpendicularly on the grill.

SLATE-GRILLED DIVER SCALLOPS

This technique is one of the many eye-opening lessons I learned from my contestants on *American Grilled.* Each competitor was allowed a single secret weapon, and in the first episode, a griller came equipped with a piece of slate. He put it directly on the grill and got it wicked hot. This was his personal technique for searing his meat. At the end of the show, I was surprised with a new customized slate in my gift bag, which became the tool for my weekend experiment of grilling fish and scallops.

SERVES 4
HANDS-ON 6 min.
TOTAL 21 min.

1   piece clean, seasoned natural slate tray (about 8 x 12 inches)
16 oz. dry-packed diver scallops

Kosher salt
Freshly ground black pepper
½   cup blended cooking oil
My Meunière Sauce

1. Light charcoal grill, or preheat gas grill to 350° to 400° (**medium-high**). When coals or grill are hot, place piece of slate on cooking grate; heat at least 15 minutes.

2. Remove scallops from packaging, and place on paper towels; pat with additional paper towels until completely dry. Season scallops with salt and pepper.

3. Brush hot slate with oil. Place the scallops on slate, making sure they do not touch each other. Sear 2 minutes on each side or just until scallops are opaque. Remove from grill, and serve with My Meunière Sauce.

MY MEUNIÈRE SAUCE

Makes: ⅓ cup   Hands-on: 2 min.   Total: 2 min.

¼   cup unsalted butter, cut into 6 pieces
2   Tbsp. chopped fresh flat-leaf parsley

2   tsp. drained capers
1   Tbsp. lemon juice

1. Place butter in a skillet over medium-high heat, and cook 1 to 2 minutes or until golden brown. Remove from heat, and stir in parsley, capers, and lemon juice.

GRILLED SCALLOP KABOBS

These easy kabobs are perfect for any night of the week. For even cooking, use scallops that are equal in size.

10 (6-inch) wooden skewers
20 fresh thick asparagus spears
40 sea scallops (about 1½ lb.)
¼ cup herb-flavored olive oil
    Lemon wedges

1. Soak wooden skewers in water 30 minutes. Meanwhile, light charcoal grill or preheat gas grill to 350° to 400° (**medium-high**). Snap off and discard tough ends of asparagus; cut into 2-inch pieces.

2. Thread scallops alternately with asparagus pieces onto skewers. Brush with oil.

3. Grill kabobs, covered with grill lid, 2½ minutes on each side or just until scallops are opaque. Season with salt to taste. Serve kabobs with lemon wedges.

PRIME CHOICE

Ask for "dry" scallops, which haven't been treated with chemicals to extend shelf life. Unprocessed scallops are naturally ivory or pinkish in color.

GRILLED HALIBUT WITH THREE-PEPPER RELISH

For a complete meal, pair this dish with steamed green beans tossed with olive oil, salt, and freshly ground black pepper and topped with pine nuts.

SERVES 8
HANDS-ON 20 min.
TOTAL 20 min.

RELISH:

1   yellow bell pepper, quartered
1   red bell pepper, quartered
1   orange bell pepper, quartered
    Vegetable cooking spray
2   Tbsp. chopped fresh parsley
2   Tbsp. chopped capers
1   Tbsp. olive oil
1   Tbsp. balsamic vinegar
¼   tsp. kosher salt
¼   tsp. freshly ground black pepper
1   garlic clove, minced

FISH:

1   Tbsp. olive oil
8   (6-oz.) skinless halibut fillets
2   tsp. chopped fresh thyme
¾   tsp. kosher salt
½   tsp. freshly ground black pepper

1. Prepare Relish: Light charcoal grill or preheat gas grill to 350° to 400° (**medium-high**). Coat bell pepper pieces with cooking spray. Place pepper pieces on a grill rack; grill 3 minutes on each side or until lightly charred. Remove from grill; cool slightly. Coarsely chop bell pepper pieces. Combine chopped bell peppers, parsley, and next 6 ingredients (through garlic); set aside.

2. Prepare Fish: Brush 1 Tbsp. oil evenly over fish. Sprinkle fish evenly with thyme, ¾ tsp. salt, and ½ tsp. black pepper. Place fish on grill rack; grill 4 minutes on each side or until fish flakes easily with a fork. Serve with relish.

GRILLED SHRIMP SALAD WITH SWEET TEA VINAIGRETTE

SERVES 6

HANDS-ON 16 min.

TOTAL 1 hr., 6 min.

This delightful dish is perfect to serve at a brunch. If ripe peaches aren't available, substitute sweet apples, such as honeycrisp.

1   cup coarsely chopped pecans
1   lb. peeled, jumbo raw shrimp (16/20 count)
1   Tbsp. olive oil
2   large fresh peaches, cut into 8 wedges each
1   (6-oz.) bag mixed baby salad greens
    Sweet Tea Vinaigrette
1   cup crumbled blue cheese

1. Preheat oven to 350°. Bake pecans in a single layer in a shallow pan 5 to 7 minutes or until lightly toasted and fragrant, stirring halfway through.

2. Light charcoal grill or preheat gas grill to 350° to 400° (**medium-high**). Devein shrimp, if desired, and toss with oil. Grill shrimp, covered with grill lid, 2 to 3 minutes on each side or just until shrimp turn pink. Grill peach wedges 1 to 2 minutes on each side or until grill marks appear.

3. Toss salad greens with Sweet Tea Vinaigrette. Season with salt and pepper to taste, and top with grilled shrimp, grilled peaches, blue cheese, and baked pecans. Serve immediately.

SWEET TEA VINAIGRETTE

Makes: about ¾ cup   Hands-on: 10 min.   Total: 40 min.

1   cup sweetened tea
2   Tbsp. cider vinegar
¼   tsp. honey
¼   tsp. Dijon mustard
    Pinch of table salt
6   Tbsp. canola oil

1. Bring tea to a boil in a saucepan over medium-low heat; reduce heat to low, and simmer 9 to 10 minutes or until reduced to ⅓ cup. Remove from heat; cool 20 minutes. Whisk in vinegar, honey, mustard, and salt. Whisk in canola oil in a slow, steady stream.

GRILLED HEAD-ON
NEW ORLEANS–STYLE BBQ SHRIMP

The original story behind this recipe started with Chef Pascal Manale, of the famous century-old restaurant, Pascale's Manale. A customer came in after a trip to Chicago and described the most incredible shrimp dish he'd ever tasted. So in his NOLA-bred culinary style, Chef sautéed the shrimp in garlic, Worcestershire sauce, black pepper, and a lot of butter. It was nothing like the dish in Chicago, the man told him. It was far better.

SERVES 6
HANDS-ON 28 min.
TOTAL 58 min.

6   (12-inch) wooden skewers
2   lb. unpeeled, raw Gulf shrimp
¼   cup olive oil, divided
10 Tbsp. butter, divided
1   tsp. whole black peppercorns
2   bay leaves
3   Tbsp. minced garlic cloves
2   Tbsp. chopped fresh rosemary
½   cup Worcestershire sauce
½   tsp. freshly ground black pepper
1   French bread baguette, sliced
4   Tbsp. extra virgin olive oil
    Table salt

1. Soak skewers in warm water 20 to 30 minutes. Peel shrimp, keeping heads on; reserve shells. Heat 2 Tbsp. olive oil and 2 Tbsp. butter in a pan over medium-high heat. Add shells, peppercorns, and bay leaves; cook 3 minutes or until shells change color. Add 2 cups water; increase heat, and simmer 10 to 12 minutes. Remove from heat; pour through a fine wire-mesh strainer into a bowl. Discard solids, and reserve stock.

2. Light charcoal grill or preheat gas grill to 350° to 400° (medium-high). Thread shrimp on skewers. Heat remaining 2 Tbsp. olive oil in pan over medium-high heat 1 minute. Add garlic; cook 1 minute. Reduce heat to medium; add rosemary, and cook 2 minutes. Add Worcestershire sauce, pepper, and 1 cup reserved shrimp stock; increase heat, and simmer until reduced by half. Brush some of sauce over shrimp, reserving remaining sauce. Place skewers on cooking grate; grill 2 minutes on each side.

3. Slice bread; brush with extra virgin olive oil, and season with salt. Grill until toasted. Reheat remaining sauce over medium-high heat; whisk in remaining 8 Tbsp. butter, 2 Tbsp. at a time. Place 1 skewer of shrimp on each serving plate, top with sauce, and serve with bread.

GRILLED CHILLED SHRIMP ROLLS

SERVES 4 to 6
HANDS-ON 10 min.
TOTAL 40 min.

This is my take on the classic New England lobster roll. Serve this buttery, rich sandwich with a crisp, cold Sam Adams beer.

1½ lb. peeled, deveined raw Gulf shrimp
1 Tbsp. olive oil
  Kosher salt
  Freshly ground black pepper
½ cup mayonnaise (such as Duke's)
1 Tbsp. Creole mustard
½ tsp. celery seeds
¼ tsp. ground red pepper
6 dashes hot sauce (such as Crystal)
¼ cup chopped green onions
½ cup finely diced red onion
4 to 6 potato hot dog rolls
  Butter, melted

1. Light charcoal grill or preheat gas grill to 350° to 400° (**medium-high**). Toss shrimp with oil in a small bowl; season with salt and pepper. Place shrimp on cooking grate, and grill 2 minutes; turn and grill an additional 2 minutes. Remove shrimp from grill; cover and chill 30 minutes.

2. Combine mayonnaise, mustard, celery seeds, red pepper, hot sauce, green onions, and red onion; mix well. Chop cooled shrimp, and add to mayonnaise mixture; cover and chill until ready to use.

3. Brush inside of each roll with melted butter, and place on cooking grate; grill until lightly toasted. Remove toasted rolls from grill, and fill with shrimp mixture.

CARIBBEAN SHRIMP KABOBS

Citrus juices have an enzyme that begins to cook the shrimp if it sits too long, so don't marinate more than 30 minutes.

1   cup fresh orange juice
¼   cup fresh lime juice
¼   cup chopped fresh cilantro
¼   cup olive oil
½   tsp. table salt
½   tsp. chili powder
4   garlic cloves, minced
1½ lb. peeled, large raw shrimp with tails, deveined
4   (12-inch) wooden or metal skewers
    Garnishes: orange slices, lime wedges

1. Whisk together first 7 ingredients in a large shallow dish or zip-top plastic freezer bag; add shrimp. Cover or seal, and chill 30 minutes. Soak wooden skewers in water 30 minutes (omit if using metal skewers).

2. Light charcoal grill or preheat gas grill to 350° to 400° (**medium-high**). Remove shrimp from marinade; reserve marinade. Thread shrimp onto skewers.

3. Grill shrimp, covered with grill lid, 2 minutes on each side or just until shrimp turn pink. Meanwhile, bring reserved marinade to a boil in a small saucepan, and cook 5 minutes. Remove from heat; drizzle over grilled shrimp.

David's
TIPS

Skewer the shrimp so they touch each other. It will prevent them from drying out and allows for easier basting.

GRILLED SHRIMP KABOBS AND SMOKY GRILLED-CORN GRITS

SERVES 4 to 6
HANDS-ON 26 min.
TOTAL 29 min.

Shrimp and grits is a classic combination. Kick it up a notch with canned chipotle peppers in adobo sauce, dried, smoked jalapeños swimming in a tangy and sweet red sauce.

2   ears fresh corn
1   tsp. table salt
1   cup uncooked quick-cooking grits
1   cup (4 oz.) shredded Cheddar cheese
2   tsp. minced canned chipotle pepper in adobo sauce
½   cup olive oil
¼   cup fresh lemon juice
1   garlic clove, pressed
½   tsp. freshly ground black pepper
1   lb. peeled, jumbo raw shrimp with tails, deveined
16 (6-inch) metal skewers
1   pt. grape tomatoes
½   (8-oz.) package fresh mushrooms, quartered
1   small green bell pepper, cut into 1-inch pieces
⅓   cup chopped fresh cilantro

1. Light charcoal grill or preheat gas grill to 350° to 400° (**medium-high**). Grill corn, covered with grill lid, 10 minutes or until done, turning once. Cut kernels from cobs. Discard cobs.

2. Bring salt and 4 cups water to a boil in a medium saucepan over medium-high heat. Gradually whisk in grits. Cook, stirring occasionally, 8 minutes or until thickened. Stir in corn kernels, cheese, and chipotle pepper. Cover and keep warm.

3. Stir together olive oil and next 3 ingredients in a large bowl. Toss shrimp with olive oil mixture; let stand at room temperature 3 minutes.

4. Remove shrimp from marinade, discarding marinade. Thread shrimp onto skewers alternately with tomatoes, mushrooms, and bell peppers.

5. Grill kabobs, covered with grill lid, 4 to 5 minutes on each side or just until shrimp turn pink. Serve kabobs with grits, and sprinkle with cilantro just before serving.

MANGO-CHILI GRILLED SHRIMP

Tropical flavors pair perfectly with charred shrimp. Be sure to watch the shrimp to prevent them from overcooking.

SERVES 6 to 8
HANDS-ON 10 min.
TOTAL 18 min.

1   large mango, peeled and cubed
¼   cup loosely packed fresh mint leaves
1   tsp. lime zest
4   Tbsp. fresh lime juice
2   Tbsp. bottled sweet chili sauce
1   Tbsp. grated fresh ginger
2   garlic cloves, minced
1   tsp. dried crushed red pepper
1   tsp. olive oil
½   tsp. kosher salt
½   tsp. freshly ground black pepper
2   lb. peeled, large raw shrimp, deveined

1. Light charcoal grill or preheat gas grill to 350° to 400° (**medium-high**). Process first 11 ingredients in a food processor 15 seconds or until combined. Stir together shrimp and ½ cup mango mixture; let stand 5 minutes. Remove shrimp from marinade; discard marinade.

2. Grill shrimp, covered with grill lid, 2 to 3 minutes on each side or just until shrimp turn pink. Toss shrimp with 4 to 6 Tbsp. mango mixture. Serve with remaining mango mixture.

David's TIPS

Make the mango mixture ahead of time and store in the refrigerator until ready to use.

CAST-IRON WOOD-GRILLED LITTLENECK CLAMS

I prefer to use wood or charcoal for this recipe, but if you only have a gas grill, place the clams in a cast-iron Dutch oven and place on top of the grill grate. Proceed with the recipe, but check the clams after 20 minutes.

SERVES 8
HANDS-ON 20 min.
TOTAL 1 hr., 20 min.

5   lb. littleneck clams, scrubbed
2   shallots, peeled and sliced
1   lemon, cut into ¼-inch slices
1   oz. fresh whole thyme leaves
1   cup dry white wine
4   Tbsp. unsalted butter, cut into ½-inch cubes
    Kosher salt
1   French bread baguette, sliced
¼   cup extra virgin olive oil

1. Build and light a wood fire in a charcoal grill or a fire pit with a wrought-iron hanging rod; allow fire to burn 20 to 30 minutes before preparing clams. Combine clams, shallots, lemon slices, thyme leaves, wine, butter, and salt to taste in a 12-inch cast-iron pot with a hanging handle and lid.

2. Create a "nest" for the pot in center of wood pile, and place covered pot directly on top of the fire. Close grill lid, and cook 20 minutes; if using a fire pit, hook covered pot onto rod directly over fire, and cook 25 to 30 minutes. Lift pot lid, and check to make sure clams are open and steamy hot; discard any clams that are not open.

3. Brush bread slices with oil; place on cooking grate, and grill until toasted. Serve clams in bowls with toasted bread.

PRIME CHOICE

If any of the clams do not open after the allotted cooking time, discard them.

SALADS AND SIDES

I THINK THERE'S SOMETHING SINGULARLY APPEALING in seeing an array of colorful vegetables laid across a grill. I recently developed a newfound admiration for veggies. It is not hard becoming a champion of an organic vegetable diet when visiting a local farmers' market and meeting the cast of characters who so passionately tend their crops, exploring how they cultivated so many ripe, colorful varieties, each with its own roots. As I became an avid griller, I discovered how just a lick from the flame and a whisper of smoke can add new layers of complexity to vegetables, bestowing on them new personalities and enhancing their culinary expressions.

My mother was careful to serve us "meat-plus-two" dinners each night, dutifully plating a carb and a vegetable beside the protein. We did not pay special attention to the cooked spinach or green beans as they were presented with no immense creativity or flavor. We didn't shop at the farmers' markets in New Orleans. As we became smarter shoppers and armed with my knowledge as a trained chef, I discovered the taste of vegetables for the first time. I encourage my family to do the same in supporting their local farmers' market.

As you will discover in the pages that follow, using grilling alone as a cooking medium opens the door to many creative preparations for vegetables. The meat-loving culture has interestingly changed its perception and now needs no convincing that vegetables are worth the time it takes to heat them up on the grill.

Cast-Iron Honey-Glazed Carrots, page 262

SMOKY CHOPPED SALAD WITH AVOCADO

SERVES 6

HANDS-ON 20 min.

TOTAL 21 min.

This is my take on the classic chopped Cobb salad. Legend states that this salad originated from the Brown Derby restaurant in Hollywood. I've added even more fresh California flavors to this iconic dish.

¾ cup buttermilk

¼ cup sour cream

2 Tbsp. freshly grated Parmesan cheese

2 Tbsp. chopped fresh chives

1 Tbsp. chopped fresh basil

1 Tbsp. fresh lemon juice

2 to 3 dashes of Worcestershire sauce

1 to 2 dashes of hot sauce

1 small garlic clove, pressed

Vegetable cooking spray

2 ripe avocados, peeled and halved

3 romaine lettuce hearts, cut in half lengthwise

½ cup thinly sliced radishes

½ cup crumbled blue cheese

1. Whisk together first 9 ingredients in a medium bowl, whisking until smooth; add salt and pepper to taste.

2. Coat cold cooking grate with cooking spray, and place on grill. Light charcoal grill or preheat gas grill to 350° to 400° (**medium-high**). Lightly coat cut sides of avocados and lettuce with cooking spray; season with salt and pepper. Grill avocado halves and lettuce, cut sides down and covered with grill lid, 1 minute or until grill marks appear.

3. Slice avocados. Chop lettuce, and arrange on a platter. Top with avocado, radishes, and blue cheese. Drizzle with dressing, and season with salt and pepper to taste.

TORTELLONI-AND-GRILLED VEGETABLE SALAD

Versatile tortelloni pairs well with any grilled fresh vegetable, so use what you have on hand or what looks best at the farmers' market.

SERVES 6
HANDS-ON 15 min.
TOTAL 40 min.

3   medium zucchini, cut in half lengthwise (about ¾ lb.)
1   (8-oz.) package sweet mini bell peppers, trimmed and seeded
1   (20-oz.) package refrigerated cheese-and-spinach tortelloni
½   cup Lemon-Shallot Vinaigrette
1   cup torn fresh basil leaves

1. Light charcoal grill or preheat gas grill to 350° to 400° (medium-high). Toss zucchini and peppers with desired amount of salt and pepper.

2. Grill vegetables, covered with grill lid, 4 to 5 minutes on each side or until tender. Remove from grill; let stand 5 minutes. Coarsely chop.

3. Prepare tortelloni according to package directions. Toss together warm tortelloni, grilled vegetables, and Lemon-Shallot Vinaigrette. Add salt and pepper to taste. Serve warm or at room temperature; sprinkle with basil just before serving.

LEMON-SHALLOT VINAIGRETTE

Makes: about 2 cups   Hands-on: 5 min.   Total: 10 min.

½   cup fresh lemon juice
1   minced shallot
1   cup olive oil
¼   cup minced fresh flat-leaf parsley
1   Tbsp. honey
1   Tbsp. whole grain Dijon mustard

1. Stir together lemon juice and minced shallot; let stand 5 minutes. Whisk in oil, parsley, honey, and mustard. Add salt and pepper to taste. Refrigerate in an airtight container up to 1 week.

GRAIN SALAD WITH GRILLED SHRIMP AND SWEET PEPPERS

SERVES 2
HANDS-ON 30 min.
TOTAL 50 min.

Bulgur is wheat that's been parboiled, dried, and cracked into nibbly bits. It cooks fast and is very versatile.

4 (8-inch) wooden or metal skewers
¾ cup uncooked bulgur wheat
5½ Tbsp. olive oil, divided
1¼ tsp. kosher salt, divided
¾ tsp. freshly ground black pepper, divided
1 lb. peeled, medium-size raw shrimp, deveined
8 oz. mini bell peppers
1 bunch green onions
4½ tsp. fresh lemon juice
⅓ cup coarsely chopped fresh flat-leaf parsley

1. Light charcoal grill or preheat gas grill to 350° to 400° (**medium-high**). Soak wooden skewers in water for 30 minutes (omit if using metal skewers).

2. Cook bulgur according to package directions. Toss together cooked bulgur, 2 Tbsp. oil, ½ tsp. salt, and ½ tsp. pepper; spread on a baking sheet. Cool completely (about 15 minutes); transfer to a large bowl.

3. Toss together shrimp, 1 Tbsp. oil, ¼ tsp. salt, and remaining ¼ tsp. pepper. Thread shrimp onto skewers. Toss together peppers and 1 Tbsp. oil.

4. Grill shrimp and peppers, covered with grill lid, 2 minutes on each side or just until shrimp turn pink. Brush onions with 1½ tsp. oil, and grill, covered with grill lid, 1 minute on each side. Slice peppers; cut onions into ½-inch-long pieces.

5. Toss together bulgur mixture, peppers, onions, lemon juice, remaining 1 Tbsp. oil, and remaining ½ tsp. salt. Top with parsley and shrimp.

GRILLED PEAR SALAD

SERVES 6 to 8

HANDS-ON 25 min.

TOTAL 25 min.

Also known as the Williams pear, the Bartlett pear is the most commonly grown variety of pear in the United States. It has a bell shape and speckled green skin.

3   firm ripe Bartlett pears, cut into ½-inch-thick wedges
¼   cup red wine vinegar
½   (10-oz.) jar seedless raspberry preserves
2   Tbsp. chopped fresh basil
1   garlic clove, pressed
½   tsp. table salt
½   tsp. seasoned pepper
⅓   cup canola oil
1   (5-oz.) package gourmet mixed salad greens
½   small red onion, thinly sliced
2   cups fresh raspberries
¾   cup honey-roasted cashews
4   oz. crumbled goat cheese

1. Light charcoal grill or preheat gas grill to 350° to 400° (**medium-high**). Grill pear wedges, covered with grill lid, 1 to 2 minutes on each side or until golden.

2. Whisk together vinegar and next 5 ingredients in a small bowl; add oil in a slow, steady stream, whisking constantly until smooth.

3. Combine salad greens, next 4 ingredients, and pears in a large bowl. Drizzle with desired amount of vinaigrette, and toss to combine. Serve immediately with remaining vinaigrette.

GRILLED SHRIMP AND SPINACH SALAD

Pump up Grilled Shrimp and Spinach Salad with a colorful mix of sliced mangoes, fresh raspberries, goat cheese, and, of course, grilled shrimp.

SERVES 8
HANDS-ON 35 min.
TOTAL 1 hr., 10 min.

- 8 (12-inch) wooden skewers
- 2 lb. peeled, large raw shrimp (31/40 count)
- Basil Vinaigrette, divided
- 2 (6-oz.) packages fresh baby spinach
- 2 mangoes, peeled and sliced
- 1 small red onion, halved and sliced
- 1 (4-oz.) package goat cheese, crumbled
- 1 cup fresh raspberries

1. Light charcoal grill or preheat gas grill to 350° to 400° (**medium-high**). Soak wooden skewers in water for 30 minutes.

2. Devein shrimp, if desired. Combine shrimp and ¾ cup Basil Vinaigrette in a large shallow dish or zip-top plastic freezer bag; cover or seal, and chill 15 minutes, turning occasionally.

3. Remove shrimp from marinade; discard marinade. Thread shrimp onto skewers.

4. Grill shrimp, covered with grill lid, 2 minutes on each side or just until shrimp turn pink. Remove shrimp from skewers.

5. Toss spinach, mangoes, and onion with ¼ cup Basil Vinaigrette in a large bowl; arrange on a serving platter. Top with grilled shrimp. Sprinkle with crumbled goat cheese and raspberries. Serve with remaining Basil Vinaigrette.

BASIL VINAIGRETTE

Makes: 1½ cups   Hands-on: 5 min.   Total: 5 min.

- ½ cup chopped fresh basil
- ½ cup raspberry vinegar
- 2 garlic cloves, minced
- 1 Tbsp. brown sugar
- 2 tsp. Dijon mustard
- ½ tsp. table salt
- ½ tsp. dried crushed red pepper
- 1 cup olive oil

1. Whisk together first 7 ingredients until blended. Add oil in a slow, steady stream, whisking constantly until smooth.

GRILLED BABY ROMAINE SALAD WITH CHARRED LEMON VINAIGRETTE AND GRILLED CROUTONS

SERVES 6

HANDS-ON 11 min.

TOTAL 18 min.

Grilling greens is a great way to invigorate a tired salad. For this dish, just slightly char the ends of the lettuce, but maintain the crispy texture. Toss the romaine hearts with the dressing while they're still hot to really make the flavors pop.

2 lemons

1 tsp. Dijon mustard

1 Tbsp. minced shallot

2 tsp. honey

　 Kosher salt

　 Freshly ground black pepper

½ cup vegetable oil

6 romaine lettuce hearts

¼ cup olive oil, divided

1 French bread baguette, cut lengthwise into 6 (6- to 8-inch) slices

4 oz. shaved Parmigiano-Reggiano cheese

1. Light charcoal grill or preheat gas grill to 350° to 400° (**medium-high**). Cut lemons lengthwise, and place, cut sides down, on cooking grate; grill 5 to 6 minutes or until grill marks and a bit of charring appear. Remove lemon halves from grill, and let stand 5 minutes; squeeze juice through a fine wire-mesh strainer into a bowl, and discard seeds and rest of lemons. Whisk in mustard, shallot, honey, salt, and pepper; whisk vigorously while slowly adding ½ cup vegetable oil. Set mixture aside.

2. Pull old leaves off each romaine heart, and trim top, leaving bottom intact; rinse well with cold water, and pat dry with paper towels. Cut romaine hearts in half lengthwise, and drizzle with 2 Tbsp. olive oil to prevent burning. Place on cooking grate, and grill until nicely charred. Remove from grill, and cool 5 minutes.

3. Brush bread slices with remaining 2 Tbsp. olive oil; sprinkle with salt, and place on cooking grate. Grill until grill marks appear and bread is toasted. Remove from grill, and cool. Place each bread slice on a salad plate. Place an open-faced grilled romaine heart on top, and drizzle liberally with vinaigrette. Sprinkle salads evenly with shaved Parmigiano-Reggiano cheese; serve immediately.

FIRED-ROASTED SMOKED LEEKS

After shooting the final episode of *American Grilled,* we had a lot of leftover produce that we threw on the grill. It was filmed at Jamison Farm, so I brought my La Caja China barbecue with me to roast a whole lamb for the closing party. The show's culinary director, Clifford, took out a bunch of leeks and threw them into the hot coals. We peeled off the blackened outer layer to reveal a delicious oozing creamy center. The method is so simple and yet the end result is so extraordinary. Thanks, Cliff!

> **SERVES 6**
> **HANDS-ON** 5 min.
> **TOTAL** 35 min.

Hickory wood chips, soaked
6   leeks, trimmed and washed
½   cup extra virgin olive oil
Kosher salt
Freshly ground black pepper

1. Light charcoal grill. Once coals are gray, sprinkle with wood chips. Place 2 leeks in center of each of 3 large sheets of aluminum foil; drizzle oil evenly over leeks, and season with salt and pepper. Bring up sides of foil over leeks; double fold top and side edges to seal, making 3 packets.

2. Place packets directly on coals, and sprinkle a couple of coals on top; grill 30 minutes. Remove from grill, and carefully unwrap. Peel back charred pieces of leeks to uncover the soft, butter-like core.

GRILLED CORN WITH HERBED COTIJA CHEESE

SERVES 6

HANDS-ON 36 min.

TOTAL 36 min.

Fresh grilled corn is a summer staple, and we've devised a delicious way to top it.

6   ears fresh corn
    Kitchen string
4   Tbsp. butter, melted
    Herbed Cotija Cheese
    Lime wedges

1. Light charcoal grill or preheat gas grill to 350° to 400° (**medium-high**). Pull back husks from ears of corn; remove and discard silks. Tie husks together with kitchen string to form a handle. Soak corn in cold salted water to cover 10 minutes; drain.

2. Grill corn, covered with grill lid, 15 minutes or until golden brown, turning occasionally.

3. Brush corn with melted butter; sprinkle with Herbed Cotija Cheese. Serve with lime wedges.

HERBED COTIJA CHEESE:

Makes: 1¼ cups   Hands-on: 5 min.   Total: 5 min.

1   cup crumbled Cotija cheese   1   tsp. chili powder
2   Tbsp. chopped fresh cilantro 1   tsp. lime zest
2   Tbsp. chopped fresh chives

1. Toss together all ingredients until combined.

CAST-IRON—GRILLED HONEY GLAZED CARROTS

SERVES 6
HANDS-ON 11 min.
TOTAL 11 min.

I created this recipe as a way to get my boys to eat their vegetables. It started out with just honey and butter and evolved, as they got older, with the addition of savory spices like cumin. Making these in a cast-iron skillet on the grill adds even more depth of flavor to the carrots, a basic vegetable that can be transformed with a little imagination.

1   lb. baby carrots, peeled
    Extra virgin olive oil
3   Tbsp. unsalted butter
3   Tbsp. wildflower honey
1   tsp. whole cumin seeds
    Kosher salt

1. Light charcoal grill or preheat gas grill to 350° to 400° (**medium-high**). Toss together peeled carrots and oil, and place carrots on cooking grate; grill, turning frequently, 5 minutes or until slightly tender and grill marks and browning appear.

2. Place a cast-iron skillet on the cooking grate; add butter, honey, and cumin seeds. When butter melts, add carrots, and cook 5 to 6 minutes or until glaze begins to coat the carrots. Sprinkle with salt, and remove from grill.

David's TIPS

Before adding the honey, check the carrots to be sure they're tender. The honey will only take a few seconds to begin thickening and darkening in color, so if you're not careful, it can quickly go from caramelized to burnt.

GRILL-SMOKED SUMMER PEAS

Here's a smart new smoky spin on baked beans that substitutes field peas or beans for traditional white beans. Try using a mix of peas and beans, such as crowders, lady peas, and butter beans.

SERVES 6
HANDS-ON 45 min.
TOTAL 2 hr., 25 min.

1   cup hickory wood chips
    Vegetable cooking spray
1   lb. fresh shelled field peas or beans (about 4 cups)
4   cups boiling water
4   fresh thyme sprigs
1   garlic bulb, cut in half crosswise
1   bay leaf
4   firm medium-size beefsteak tomatoes, cored
6   bacon slices, chopped
6   garlic cloves, chopped
3   Tbsp. molasses
2   Tbsp. Dijon mustard
2   Tbsp. apple cider vinegar
2   tsp. kosher salt
1   tsp. ground black pepper

1. Soak wood chips in water 30 minutes; drain. Coat cold cooking grate with cooking spray, and place on grill. Light 1 side of charcoal grill or preheat gas grill to 400° to 500° (**high**); leave other side unlit. Place wood chips in center of a 12-inch square piece of heavy-duty aluminum foil; wrap to form a packet. Pierce several holes in packet; place directly over heat.

2. Combine peas or beans and next 4 ingredients in a 13- x 9-inch disposable foil pan. Place pan over unlit side of grill, and grill, covered with grill lid, 1 hour or until tender, stirring occasionally. Drain, reserving ¾ cup cooking liquid. Discard thyme sprigs, garlic bulb, and bay leaf.

3. Halve tomatoes, and grill, covered with grill lid, 2 minutes on each side. Cool 10 minutes. Discard skins; chop tomatoes.

4. Cook bacon in a large saucepan over medium heat, stirring often, 4 minutes or until crisp. Remove bacon from pan, and drain, reserving 2 Tbsp. drippings. Return reserved drippings and bacon to pan, and add chopped garlic; sauté 30 seconds. Stir in tomatoes, molasses, and next 2 ingredients; bring to a simmer. Reduce heat to low, and simmer, stirring often, 5 minutes. Stir peas, salt, pepper, and ¾ cup reserved cooking liquid into tomato mixture; cook, stirring often, 10 minutes or until slightly thickened. Adjust seasoning with more vinegar, molasses, salt, and pepper, if desired.

GRILLED BOK CHOY

Round out a meal by grilling this simple veggie alongside fish or chicken.

SERVES 6
HANDS-ON 9 min.
TOTAL 9 min.

¼ cup butter, melted
1 Tbsp. Pork Dry Rub (page 25)
2 garlic cloves, minced
6 heads baby bok choy, halved

1. Light charcoal grill or preheat gas grill to 350° to 400° (**medium-high**). Stir together butter, Pork Dry Rub, and garlic in a small bowl.

2. Grill bok choy, covered with grill lid, 2 minutes on each side or until edges are slightly charred, basting often with butter mixture.

GRILLED MEXICAN CORN SALAD

Here's an off-the-cob play on a popular Mexican street dish.

SERVES 6 to 8
HANDS-ON 25 min.
TOTAL 40 min.

3 limes, divided
8 large ears fresh yellow corn, husks removed
3 Tbsp. mayonnaise
⅔ cup crumbled feta or Cotija cheese
⅓ cup sliced fresh chives

1. Cut 2 limes in half, and squeeze juice from lime halves to equal about ¼ cup.

2. Light charcoal grill or preheat gas grill to 400° to 500° (**high**). Brush corn with mayonnaise; sprinkle with desired amount of salt and pepper. Grill corn, covered with grill lid, 10 to 12 minutes or until done, turning occasionally (kernels may char and pop).

3. Hold each grilled cob upright on a cutting board, and carefully cut downward, cutting kernels from cob; discard cobs. Place kernels in a large bowl, and stir in cheese, chives, and lime juice. Cut remaining lime into 4 wedges, and serve with corn salad.

GO-TO MIXED VEGGIES

SERVES 6
HANDS-ON 10 min.
TOTAL 10 min.

When I aimlessly food shop in the produce section, I often wind up with a plethora of vegetables. For as long as I've been grilling, I have a simple method that can be applied to almost any vegetable you have on hand. Cut them in half, toss with olive oil, salt, and pepper, and grill them until they're soft and slightly charred. I like cutting the vegetables into meaty chunks and tossing them with balsamic vinegar or fresh herbs, like parsley and rosemary. That step is an added bonus, but the true stars are the basic grilled vegetables.

2   medium zucchini

2   medium yellow squash

1   whole red onion, peeled and sliced into ½-inch rings

3   (4- to 5-inch) whole portobello mushrooms, stemmed and cleaned

½   cup extra virgin olive oil

     Kosher salt

     Freshly ground black pepper

½   cup chopped fresh flat-leaf parsley

2   Tbsp. balsamic vinegar

1. Light 1 side of charcoal grill or preheat gas grill to 350° to 400° (**medium-high**); leave other side unlit. Trim ends of zucchini and squash, and cut in half lengthwise. Drizzle zucchini, squash, onion rings, and mushrooms with oil, and season with salt and pepper. Place vegetables on cooking grate over lit coals, and close grill lid. Grill 5 to 10 minutes or until cooked through; if veggies brown too quickly, move them to unlit side of grill.

2. Remove vegetables from grill, and place on a cutting board; slice zucchini and squash on the bias, chop onion rings, and slice mushrooms into ½-inch slices. Place all vegetables in a bowl; add parsley and vinegar before serving.

David's TIPS

This is what I call an "in a pinch" dish. Cutting vegetables in half makes them cook much more quickly than they would whole. You can make this with whatever you already have in your refrigerator.

GRILLED SMOKED CAULIFLOWER

Cauliflower steaks have begun appearing on menus across the country. The thick stem and dense florets give the cruciferous veggie a meaty quality. When grilling the cauliflower, it's best to take it off the grill just when the stalk is tender enough to eat and before the florets get too soft.

SERVES 4 to 6
HANDS-ON 10 min.
TOTAL 21 min.

2   large heads cauliflower
5½ Tbsp. extra virgin olive oil, divided
     Kosher salt
     Freshly ground black pepper
     Apple wood chips, soaked
2   Tbsp. chopped fresh flat-leaf parsley
½   cup sliced almonds, toasted

1. Light charcoal grill or preheat gas grill to 350° to 400° (**medium-high**); leave other side unlit. Remove leaves from cauliflower, and trim sides and stem ends. Stand each head of cauliflower on flat end, and cut directly down to make 3 to 4 thick slices ("steaks"); reserve any florets that fall off for another use. Brush both sides of each cauliflower slice evenly using 4 Tbsp. oil; season with salt and pepper.

2. Sprinkle wood chips over hot coals. Place cauliflower slices on cooking grate; grill, covered with grill lid, 6 to 7 minutes. Turn cauliflower slices, and grill, covered with grill lid, 5 more minutes. Remove from grill, and place on serving platter; drizzle with remaining 1½ Tbsp. oil, and sprinkle with parsley and almonds before serving.

David's TIPS

To get more "steaks" out of a head of cauliflower, choose those with thicker stems. Collect the loose florets that remain and grill them in a foil packet so they too get the flavor elements from the grill, and serve them alongside the steaks.

CHARRED OKRA

SERVES 6
HANDS-ON 15 min.
TOTAL 1 hr., 30 min.

Garam masala lends Indian flavor to grilled okra, making it a great way to enjoy okra without frying it. These little bite-sized green vegetables are extraordinarily versatile. You can throw just about anything their way, but even the most basic combination of olive oil, salt, and pepper turns them into a delicious side dish.

3   limes
2   lb. medium-size fresh okra
1   Tbsp. garam masala
2   Tbsp. olive oil
2   garlic cloves, minced
1½ tsp. kosher salt
1½ tsp. freshly ground black pepper
¼   cup chopped fresh cilantro

1. Grate zest from 2 limes to equal 2½ Tbsp.; squeeze juice from same 2 limes to equal 5 Tbsp. Cut remaining lime into 8 wedges.

2. Toss together okra, next 5 ingredients, lime zest, and lime juice in a bowl. Cover and chill 1 hour.

3. Light charcoal grill or preheat gas grill to 350° to 400° (**medium-high**). Remove okra from marinade; discard marinade. Grill okra, without grill lid, 10 to 15 minutes or just until tender and lightly charred, turning often. Sprinkle with cilantro; serve with lime wedges.

GRILLED SWEET POTATOES

SERVES 6
HANDS-ON 20 min.
TOTAL 20 min.

Use a mandoline set to ½ inch to evenly slice the sweet potato into planks.

⅓ cup olive oil
1 Tbsp. minced shallot
1 Tbsp. chopped fresh rosemary
1 tsp. kosher salt
1 tsp. coarsely ground black pepper
3 large sweet potatoes, peeled and cut into ½-inch-thick slices
½ cup crumbled blue cheese

1. Light charcoal grill or preheat gas grill to 350° to 400° (**medium-high**). Stir together first 5 ingredients in a small bowl, and brush on sweet potato slices.

2. Grill, covered with grill lid, 3 to 4 minutes on each side or until tender. Place potatoes on a serving platter; sprinkle with blue cheese.

STEP-BY-STEP

1. Use a basting brush to coat the sweet potato rounds.

2. An offset metal spatula makes it easier to flip the sweet potato rounds.

CHARRED EGGPLANT WITH MISO DRESSING

You can find miso, a Japanese staple with a slightly salty, pungent flavor, in the international or refrigerated aisle of your grocery store.

SERVES 6
HANDS-ON 25 min.
TOTAL 25 min.

⅓ cup mayonnaise

2 Tbsp. white miso

1 Tbsp. fresh lime juice

⅛ tsp. freshly ground black pepper

2 large eggplants (about 2 lb.)

¼ cup olive oil

¼ cup torn fresh cilantro leaves

1. Light charcoal grill or preheat gas grill to 350° to 400° (**medium-high**). Stir together first 4 ingredients in a small bowl.

2. Cut eggplants lengthwise into ¾-inch-thick slices. Brush each slice with oil, and sprinkle with desired amount of salt and pepper.

3. Grill eggplant slices, without grill lid, 5 minutes on each side or until slightly charred and tender. Arrange on a serving platter, and drizzle with desired amount of dressing; top with cilantro. Serve immediately with remaining dressing.

GRILLED ARTICHOKES

SERVES 8
HANDS-ON 32 min.
TOTAL 52 min.

Prepare the artichokes the day before and place them in zip-top plastic bags in the refrigerator.

4   artichokes, halved and boiled (see Step-By-Step below)
2   lemons, halved
¾   cup olive oil
1   tsp. kosher salt
½   tsp. freshly ground black pepper
4   garlic cloves, minced
¼   cup freshly grated Parmesan cheese

1. Light charcoal grill or preheat gas grill to 350° to 400° (**medium-high**). Whisk together oil, salt, pepper, and garlic. Grill prepared artichokes, cut sides down, covered with grill lid, 6 minutes. Turn; spoon olive oil mixture over artichoke halves.

2. Grill, covered with grill lid, 6 more minutes or until slightly charred and lower leaves pull out easily. At same time, grill lemons, cut sides down, covered with lid, 5 minutes or until slightly charred.

3. Place artichokes, cut sides up, on a serving platter; squeeze grilled lemons over artichokes, and sprinkle with Parmesan cheese.

STEP-BY-STEP

1. Wash artichokes by plunging in cold water. Cut off stem ends, and trim about ½ inch from top of each artichoke. Remove any loose bottom leaves.

2. Trim one-fourth off top of each outer leaf with scissors. Cut each artichoke in half lengthwise. Rub edges with cut lemons, reserving lemons.

3. Remove thistle with a spoon. Boil artichokes over high heat, covered, for 20 minutes or just until barely tender.

BLUE CHEESE–STUFFED PORTOBELLO MUSHROOMS

SERVES 4
HANDS-ON 27 min.
TOTAL 27 min.

I'm a big mushroom guy. I could probably fill an entire cookbook solely with grilled mushroom recipes. Their soft, meaty flesh absorbs flavors like a sponge, which translates so well on the grill. Beefy portobellos are the vehicles here that tie together the creamy, salty blue cheese; sweet onions; and savory, textured breadcrumbs.

3   Tbsp. extra virgin olive oil, divided
4   Tbsp. Worcestershire sauce, divided
½   tsp. kosher salt
4   (4- to 5-inch) portobello mushrooms, stemmed and cleaned
½   cup finely diced onion
1   clove garlic, minced
1   Tbsp. fresh rosemary, chopped
½   cup crumbled blue cheese
½   cup grated Parmesan cheese
½   tsp. Dijon mustard
½   cup panko (Japanese breadcrumbs)

1. Light 1 side of charcoal grill or preheat gas grill to 350° to 400° (**medium-high**); leave other side unlit. Combine 2 Tbsp. oil, 2 Tbsp. Worcestershire sauce, and salt in a small bowl, and mix well. Place mushrooms, cap sides down, on a plate, and spoon mixture on bottom sides of mushrooms; let stand 5 minutes. Place on cooking grate, cap sides up, and grill 5 minutes; turn mushrooms, and grill 2 to 3 more minutes. Remove from grill.

2. Meanwhile, pour remaining 1 Tbsp. oil into a small sauté pan, and place over medium heat; add onion, and cook 2 minutes. Add garlic, and cook 2 more minutes; remove from heat, and place mixture in a bowl. Add rosemary, cheeses, mustard, panko, and remaining 2 Tbsp. Worcestershire sauce; use a wooden spoon to mash ingredients together. Spoon stuffing evenly into mushroom caps.

3. Place stuffed mushrooms on cooking grate on unlit side of grill, just off direct heat. Open grill dampers halfway to allow airflow, and cover with grill lid. Grill mushrooms 15 minutes or until browned. Remove from grill, and serve.

GRILLED POTATO SALAD

On one episode of "American Grilled," the show's winner cooked potatoes wrapped in a foil pouch nestled in the coals. It sparked a childhood memory of when we went camping as a family. We'd cook all sorts of things directly in the fire, from cans of baked beans to potatoes. For this barbecue staple, I use skin-on baby red potatoes, which cook faster and are less starchy than a regular baking potato.

SERVES 6
HANDS-ON 25 min.
TOTAL 1 hr., 35 min.

2½ lb. small red potatoes, halved
¼ cup mayonnaise (such as Duke's)
⅓ cup prepared horseradish
1 Tbsp. Creole mustard
½ cup green onions, thinly sliced
1 Tbsp. apple cider vinegar
1 tsp. hot sauce
1 tsp. kosher salt
¼ tsp. freshly ground black pepper

1. Pile and light charcoal in center of grill. Place half of potatoes in a single layer in center of a large piece of heavy-duty aluminum foil, and pour ½ cup water over potatoes; repeat with a second piece of foil and remaining potatoes. Bring up sides of foil over potatoes; double fold top and side edges to seal, making a packet.

2. Place foil packets alongside hot coals, and grill 1 hour or until potatoes are fork-tender. Remove foil packets from grill, and cool 10 to 15 minutes.

3. Combine mayonnaise and next 7 ingredients in a large bowl, and mix well. Cut cooled potatoes into pieces, and add to mixture. Wearing gloves, use your hands or back of a wooden spoon to mash about one-third of the salad; stir to mix.

HUSH PUPPIES

Once you have this recipe down, experiment with some fun stir-ins, such as crispy bacon and diced jalapeño.

SERVES 8 to 10
HANDS-ON 25 min.
TOTAL 35 min.

Vegetable oil
1½ cups self-rising white cornmeal mix
¾   cup self-rising flour
¾   cup diced sweet onion (about ½ medium onion)
1½ Tbsp. sugar
1   large egg, lightly beaten
1¼ cups buttermilk

1. Pour oil to depth of 3 inches into a Dutch oven; heat to 375°. Combine cornmeal mix and next 3 ingredients. Add egg and buttermilk; stir just until moistened. Let stand 10 minutes.

2. Drop batter by tablespoonfuls into hot oil; fry, in 3 batches, 2 to 3 minutes on each side or until golden. Keep warm in a 200° oven.

PRIME CHOICE

Self-rising cornmeal mix has leaveners already mixed in, which makes for light and fluffy puppies.

3-BEAN BARBECUE BAKED BEANS

SERVES 8 to 10

HANDS-ON 2 hr., 34 min.

TOTAL 3 hr., 19 min., plus 8 hr. for soaking

Smoky and sweet, these beans will be your go-to side dish at your next barbecue.

¾ cup dried pinto beans
1 cup dried red kidney beans
¾ cup dried black beans
½ lb. bacon slices
½ lb. ground pork sausage
½ cup diced yellow onion
   Vegetable cooking spray
⅔ cup firmly packed dark brown sugar
1½ Tbsp. yellow mustard
1 tsp. table salt

1. Place beans in a large stockpot; cover with water to 2 inches above beans. Let soak 8 hours; drain. Bring beans and 10 cups water to a boil in stockpot. Partially cover, reduce heat, and simmer 2 hours or until beans are tender, stirring occasionally (do not drain).

2. Preheat oven to 350°. Cook bacon in a large skillet over medium-high heat 4 minutes or until crisp; remove bacon, and drain on paper towels, reserving drippings in skillet. Crumble bacon. Add sausage and onion to hot drippings in skillet; cook over medium-high heat, stirring often, 4 minutes or until sausage crumbles and is no longer pink.

3. Lightly grease an 11- x 7-inch baking dish with cooking spray. Stir ½ cup water, sugar, mustard, and salt into beans; add bacon and sausage mixture, stirring until blended. Pour into prepared baking dish. Bake, covered, at 350° for 45 minutes or until bubbly.

David's TIPS

For extra insurance, add a little baking soda to the pot of beans before simmering. The alkaline in baking soda breaks down the cell structure of the dried beans.

CLASSIC BAKED MACARONI AND CHEESE

Whisk warm milk into the flour mixture to ensure a lump-free sauce. I also recommend shredding your own cheese for a creamier texture.

SERVES 6 to 8
HANDS-ON 27 min.
TOTAL 47 min.

2   cups milk
2   Tbsp. butter
2   Tbsp. all-purpose flour
½   tsp. table salt
¼   tsp. freshly ground black pepper
1   (10-oz.) block extra-sharp Cheddar cheese, shredded
¼   tsp. ground red pepper (optional)
½   (16-oz.) package elbow macaroni, cooked
    Vegetable cooking spray

1. Preheat oven to 400°. Microwave milk at HIGH 1½ minutes. Melt butter in a large skillet or Dutch oven over medium-low heat; whisk in flour until smooth. Cook, whisking constantly, 1 minute.

2. Gradually whisk in warm milk, and cook, whisking constantly, 5 minutes or until thickened. Whisk in salt, black pepper, 1 cup shredded cheese, and, if desired, red pepper until smooth; stir in pasta.

3. Lightly grease a 2-qt. baking dish with cooking spray. Spoon pasta mixture into prepared baking dish; top with remaining cheese. Bake at 400° for 20 minutes or until golden and bubbly.

SWEET ENDINGS

I LIKE TO CALL MYSELF THE "ACCIDENTAL PASTRY CHEF." You see, my journey from punk kid without a cause in New Orleans to executive pastry chef of a restaurant group in D.C. was one of random luck and extraordinary fortune. When I was growing up, my parents sent me to stay with my Aunt Boo in Abbeville, Louisiana, whenever I'd misbehave beyond their threshold for troublemaking. As far as Aunt Boo was concerned, there was no better remedy for poor behavior than some good, clean fun in the kitchen.

That kitchen became a sacred part of my life. It's where I began my life-long journey in pursuit of making people happy through food. After dropping out of college I was guided by my Grannie's cousin to enroll in culinary school—Sclafani Cooking School in a New Orleans suburb. After graduating, I wound up on the doorstep of the Windsor Court Hotel, humbly applying for the only open position, the one for which I was least qualified: pastry chef.

Dessert is one of life's simplest joys. It's that final farewell to a meal, that little something extra that puts a smile on your face. For me, the single greatest thing about cooking is that it lets me make people happy. Dessert, in all its sugary glory, is one of the best ways to achieve that goal.

Ooey-Chewy Chocolate
Cookies, page 311

GRILLED PEACHES WITH MASCARPONE CREAM AND SORGHUM DRIZZLE

SERVES 4
HANDS-ON 15 min.
TOTAL 25 min.

As my career changed focus from pastry to overall cooking, I started adjusting the way I approached desserts. I often like to incorporate savory elements to counteract the sugar and bring more balance to the dish. Here, the mascarpone and sorghum highlight the diversity of the smoky grilled peach while still letting the pureness of the fruit steal the show.

4   peaches, halved
4   oz. pecans
4   oz. mascarpone cheese
2   Tbsp. powdered sugar
¼   cup whipping cream
8   tsp. sorghum
½   tsp. sea salt

1. Light charcoal grill or preheat gas grill to 350° to 400° (**medium-high**). Clean cooking grate. Place peach halves, skin sides down, on cooking grate, and grill until browned; turn and grill cut sides until browned and natural fruit sugars caramelize. Remove from grill.

2. Preheat oven to 325°. Place pecans on an ungreased baking sheet, and bake 10 to 12 minutes or until toasted. Remove from oven, and cool; crumble toasted pecans.

3. Beat together mascarpone cheese and 1 Tbsp. sugar at medium speed with an electric mixer or the whisk attachment of a heavy-duty stand mixer until light and fluffy. Combine cream and remaining 1 Tbsp. sugar in another bowl; beat at high speed 1 to 2 minutes or just until stiff peaks form. Fold whipped cream mixture into mascarpone mixture.

4. Place 2 grilled peach halves on each serving plate. Top with 1 Tbsp. mascarpone-cream mixture, 2 tsp. sorghum, ⅛ tsp. sea salt, and 1 oz. crumbled pecans.

David's
TIPS

Grill a few extra peaches and refrigerate them overnight in a zip-top plastic bag to make Grilled Peach BBQ Sauce (page 23).

GRILLED PLUM CROSTATA WITH PORT GLAZE

SERVES 8
HANDS-ON 24 min.
TOTAL 3 hr., 48 min.

Cream Cheese Piecrust
1¾ cups ruby port
⅔ cup sugar
2 Tbsp. red wine vinegar
Vegetable cooking spray

10 plums, halved and pitted
1½ Tbsp. canola oil
¼ tsp. ground cinnamon
3 Tbsp. sugar, divided
2 Tbsp. butter, cubed

1. Prepare Cream Cheese Piecrust.

2. Combine port, ⅔ cup sugar, and vinegar in a medium saucepan. Bring to a boil over medium-high heat; cook 25 minutes or until syrupy and reduced to 1 cup. Remove from heat, and cool completely (about 30 minutes).

3. Coat cold cooking grate with cooking spray, and place on grill. Light charcoal grill or preheat gas grill to 350° to 400° (**medium-high**). Brush plum halves with oil; sprinkle cut sides of plums with cinnamon and 2 Tbsp. sugar. Place plums on cooking grate; grill, covered with grill lid, 4 minutes on each side or until tender. Remove plums from grill; cool completely (about 30 minutes). Cut plum halves in half, and toss with 3 Tbsp. cooled port glaze.

4. Preheat oven to 400°. Roll chilled dough into a 12-inch circle on a lightly floured surface, and fold in half; transfer to an aluminum foil–lined baking sheet, and unfold. Mound plum filling in center of dough, leaving a 2-inch border. Fold dough over plum mixture; fold up sides, and dot with butter. Sprinkle with remaining 1 Tbsp. sugar. Bake for 45 minutes or until golden; cool on a wire rack. Drizzle desired amount of remaining port glaze over filling.

CREAM CHEESE PIECRUST

Makes: 1 (9-inch) piecrust Hands-on: 14 min. Total: 1 hr., 14 min.

6 Tbsp. butter, at room temperature	¼ tsp. table salt
2 oz. cream cheese, at room temperature	1¼ cups all-purpose flour
2 Tbsp. sugar	1½ Tbsp. ice water

1. Beat first 4 ingredients at medium speed with an electric mixer until creamy. Gradually add flour, beating at low speed just until blended. Add ice water, beating until mixture pulls away from sides of bowl and forms a ball. Flatten ball into a disk; cover and chill 1 hour.

SUMMER FRUIT COBBLER

SERVES 6 to 8
HANDS-ON 20 min.
TOTAL 1 hr., 25 min.

Tossing the fruit with cornstarch thickens the juices as it cooks. Serve this warm and bubbly dish with a scoop of vanilla ice cream.

Vegetable cooking spray
3   Tbsp. cornstarch
1½ cups sugar, divided
3   cups coarsely chopped, peeled fresh nectarines
2   cups fresh blueberries
1   cup fresh raspberries
½   cup butter, softened
2   large eggs
1½ cups all-purpose flour
1½ tsp. baking powder
1   (8-oz.) container sour cream
½   tsp. baking soda

1. Preheat oven to 350°. Lightly grease an 11- x 7-inch baking dish with cooking spray. Stir together cornstarch and ½ cup sugar. Toss nectarines and berries with cornstarch mixture, and spoon into prepared baking dish.

2. Beat butter at medium speed with an electric mixer until fluffy; gradually add remaining 1 cup sugar, beating well. Add eggs, 1 at a time, beating just until blended after each addition.

3. Combine flour and baking powder. Stir together sour cream and baking soda. Add flour mixture to butter mixture alternately with sour cream mixture, beginning and ending with flour mixture; beat at low speed just until blended after each addition. Spoon batter over fruit mixture.

4. Bake at 350° for 45 minutes. Shield loosely with aluminum foil to prevent excessive browning, and bake 20 to 25 more minutes or until golden brown and bubbly.

STEP-BY-STEP

1. Beating the butter and sugar until light and fluffy ensures a light biscuit.

2. Use a large serving spoon to form the biscuits.

GERMAN CHOCOLATE PIES

SERVES 12
HANDS-ON 48 min.
TOTAL 3 hr., 13 min.

This is a take on the classic German chocolate cake. Did you know that this recipe originated not from Germany, but from a woman in Texas who used Baker's German's Sweet Chocolate in her creation?

2   recipes Chocolate Pastry
1   (5-oz.) can evaporated milk
½   cup granulated sugar
¼   cup firmly packed light brown sugar
¼   cup butter
2   large egg yolks
½   cup chopped toasted pecans
1   tsp. vanilla extract
1   cup sweetened flaked coconut, toasted
⅓   cup finely chopped German chocolate

1. Prepare 2 recipes of Chocolate Pastry dough through Step 1. Preheat oven to 400°.

2. Roll each recipe of chilled dough to ⅛-inch thickness on a lightly floured surface, and cut into 6 rounds using a 4-inch round cutter. Press rounds into a (12-cup) muffin pan, forming cups. Freeze 10 minutes or until firm.

3. Bake at 400° for 12 to 15 minutes or until set. Cool in pan on a wire rack 10 minutes; remove from pan to wire rack, and cool completely (about 15 minutes).

4. Meanwhile, cook evaporated milk and next 4 ingredients in a heavy 2-qt. saucepan over medium heat, stirring constantly, 3 to 4 minutes or until butter melts and sugars dissolve. Cook, stirring constantly, 10 more minutes or until mixture is bubbly and reaches a pudding-like thickness.

5. Remove pan from heat; stir in pecans, vanilla, and ½ cup coconut. Transfer mixture to a bowl. Let stand, stirring occasionally, 45 minutes or until cooled. Spoon filling evenly into prepared shells; sprinkle with chopped chocolate and remaining ½ cup coconut.

CHOCOLATE PASTRY

Makes: 1 (10-inch) piecrust Hands-on: 10 min. Total: 1 hour, 57 min.

1	cup all-purpose flour	⅛	tsp. table salt
¾	cup powdered sugar	½	cup butter, cut into pieces
⅓	cup unsweetened cocoa	1	large egg, lightly beaten

1. Whisk together first 4 ingredients in a medium bowl until blended. Add butter, and gently rub with fingers until mixture resembles fine meal. Add egg, stirring with a fork just until dry ingredients are moistened and dough can be shaped into a ball. Flatten ball into a disk; cover and chill 1 hour.

2. Preheat oven to 400°. Roll chilled dough into a 12-inch circle on a lightly floured surface. Fit dough into a 10-inch tart pan with removable bottom; press into fluted edges. Fold any excess dough over outside of pan, and pinch to secure to pan (this will keep piecrust from sliding down pan as it bakes). Freeze 10 minutes or until firm.

3. Bake at 400° for 17 minutes or until set. Remove from oven to a wire rack; cool completely (about 20 minutes).

GRILLED POUND CAKE WITH RUM-SCENTED GRILLED PINEAPPLE

SERVES 6

HANDS-ON 25 min.

TOTAL 3 hr., 25 min., plus 8 hr. for chilling

When I was growing up, my family used to take summer vacations to Tortola in the British Virgin Islands. I loved eating the rum cake there. It gave me a warm burning sensation in my stomach, but it was so sweet and moist that I always wanted more. As an adult, I love grilling pineapple chunks and dropping them into a glass of rum, which ultimately inspired this dessert. The dense pound cake absorbs the alcohol and pineapple juices, infusing itself with flavor.

16 Tbsp. unsalted butter, softened

2 Tbsp. all-purpose flour

3 large eggs, at room temperature

¼ cup whole milk

1 vanilla bean, split and scraped

1½ cups plus 2 Tbsp. cake flour, sifted

1 tsp. baking powder

½ tsp. kosher salt

¾ cup granulated sugar

½ fresh pineapple, cut into spears

½ cup light brown sugar

½ tsp. freshly ground black pepper

¼ cup dark rum, optional

Whipped cream

1. Preheat oven to 350°. Use 2 Tbsp. butter to grease bottom and sides of a 9- x 5-inch loaf pan. Add 2 Tbsp. flour, and shake pan to evenly coat bottom and sides; tap out and discard any excess flour. Whisk together eggs, milk, and vanilla in a small bowl. Combine cake flour, baking powder, salt, and ¾ cup granulated sugar; beat at low speed with paddle attachment of an electric mixer just until blended. Add remaining 14 Tbsp. butter and half of egg mixture; continue to beat on low speed until dry ingredients are wet and almost fully incorporated. Increase speed to medium-high, and beat 30 seconds. Slowly add half of remaining egg mixture, and beat on medium-high until mixed; add remaining egg mixture, and beat on medium-high until mixed.

2. Pour batter into prepared pan, and bake 1 hour or until a long wooden pick inserted in center comes out clean. Cool in pan on a wire rack 15 minutes before removing cake from pan; remove from pan to a wire rack, and cool completely at least 45 minutes. Wrap cake in plastic wrap, and chill overnight.

3. About an hour before serving, combine pineapple spears, light brown sugar, black pepper, and rum, if desired, in a zip-top plastic freezer bag; seal bag, and gently shake to mix all ingredients. Chill at least 1 hour.

4. Meanwhile, light charcoal grill or preheat gas grill to 350° to 400° (**medium-high**). Remove pineapple spears from bag, and discard marinade. Place pineapple spears on cooking grate, and grill, turning frequently, until grill marks appear and juices start to bubble. Remove from grill.

5. Unwrap chilled cake, and slice into 6 pieces; place on cooking grate, and grill 2 to 4 minutes or until toasted (grill only 1 side of each piece). Remove cake from grill, and top each serving with 1 to 2 pineapple spears and a generous dollop of whipped cream.

IN-A-PINCH CREAM-FILLED GRILLED POUND CAKE

SERVES 4
HANDS-ON 5 min.
TOTAL 11 min.

Sometimes it is hard to make a dessert from scratch. Wow your guests with this super easy dessert that is only five ingredients. If you have homemade pound cake, that's the best, but frozen or fresh store-bought works in a pinch!

4   tablespoons pineapple cream cheese
8   (½-inch-thick) slices pound cake
    Sweetened whipped cream
    Fresh strawberries and blueberries

1. Spread pineapple cream cheese evenly over 1 side of 4 pound cake slices. Top with remaining 4 pound cake slices.

2. Light charcoal grill or preheat gas grill to 350° to 400° (**medium-high**). Grill, covered with grill lid, 2 to 3 minutes on each side. Top with whipped cream and berries. Serve immediately.

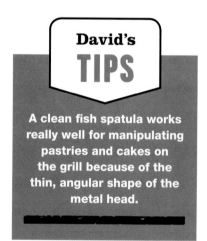

David's TIPS

A clean fish spatula works really well for manipulating pastries and cakes on the grill because of the thin, angular shape of the metal head.

GRILLED BANANA SPLITS

This recipe calls for baby bananas (also known as Oritos, Lady Fingers, and Manzanos) or small bananas that are just ripe but still firm so they'll hold their shape on the grill. If you are using a charcoal grill, place the banana halves around the outer edge to help prevent burning, and watch them carefully because they will cook fast. For easy variations, substitute other flavors of ice cream or frozen yogurt.

SERVES 6
HANDS-ON 15 min.
TOTAL 30 min.

Vegetable cooking spray
¼ cup chopped pecans
¼ cup sweetened flaked coconut
6 unpeeled baby or small bananas with green tips
6 fresh pineapple slices
1 pt. fat-free vanilla ice cream
1 pt. low-fat chocolate frozen yogurt
Garnish: chocolate sauce, maraschino cherries

1. Coat cold cooking grate with cooking spray, and place on grill. Light charcoal grill or preheat gas grill to 300° to 350° (**medium**).

2. Preheat oven to 350°. Place pecans in a single layer in a shallow pan. Place coconut in a single layer in another shallow pan. Bake pecans and coconut 7 to 8 minutes or until toasted and pecans are fragrant, stirring occasionally.

3. Peel bananas, and cut in half lengthwise; coat with cooking spray. Grill pineapple slices, covered with grill lid, 4 minutes on each side or until lightly caramelized. Grill banana halves 1 to 2 minutes on each side or until lightly caramelized.

4. Chop grilled pineapple. Arrange 2 grilled banana halves in each of 6 (8-oz.) banana-split dishes or other serving bowls. Scoop ¼ cup vanilla ice cream and ¼ cup chocolate frozen yogurt into each dish between banana slices. Top each with 1 chopped pineapple slice, 2 tsp. pecans, and 2 tsp. coconut. Serve immediately.

BUTTER CRUNCH LEMON BARS

SERVES 12

HANDS-ON 45 min.

TOTAL 45 min., plus 8 hr. for chilling

Substitute fresh orange juice and grated orange zest for lemon, if you wish. These are best served chilled.

CRUST:

⅓ cup butter, softened

¼ cup firmly packed dark brown sugar

¼ tsp. table salt

¼ tsp. ground mace or nutmeg

4.5 oz. all-purpose flour (about 1 cup)

Vegetable cooking spray

FILLING:

1 cup 1% low-fat cottage cheese

1 cup granulated sugar

2 Tbsp. all-purpose flour

1 Tbsp. grated lemon zest

3½ Tbsp. fresh lemon juice

¼ tsp. baking powder

1 large egg

1 large egg white

Powdered sugar (optional)

1. Prepare Crust: Preheat oven to 350°. Place first 4 ingredients in a large bowl, and beat at medium speed with an electric mixer until smooth. Weigh or lightly spoon 4.5 oz. (about 1 cup) flour into a dry measuring cup, and level with a knife. Add flour to butter mixture, and beat at low speed until well blended. Press crust into bottom of an 8-inch square metal baking pan coated with cooking spray. Bake at 350° for 20 minutes.

2. Prepare Filling: Place cottage cheese in a food processor; process 2 minutes or until smooth, scraping sides of bowl once. Add granulated sugar and next 6 ingredients (through egg white), and process until well blended. Pour filling over crust.

3. Bake at 350° for 25 minutes or until set (the edges will get lightly browned). Cool. Cover and chill 8 hours. Sprinkle with powdered sugar before serving, if desired.

MONKEY HILL BREAD

This banana bread is similar to the only dessert that Nana, my Aunt Boo's mother, could or would ever make. If my memory serves my taste buds correctly, it should be spongy, moist, and naturally nectarous from the over-ripe bananas. And wow, what a sweet fragrance it must deliver! This recipe is perfect for school lunches or an afternoon snack with friends.

SERVES 8
HANDS-ON 15 min.
TOTAL 2 hr., 15 min.

- 10 Tbsp. unsalted butter, softened and divided
- 1¾ cups plus 2 Tbsp. all-purpose flour, divided
- ½ tsp. ground cinnamon
- 1 tsp. baking soda
- ½ tsp. table salt
- 3 very ripe bananas
- 1 tsp. fresh lemon juice
- 3 Tbsp. whole milk
- 1 Tbsp. sour cream
- ½ cup granulated sugar
- ½ cup firmly packed dark brown sugar
- ½ tsp. vanilla extract
- 2 large eggs

1. Preheat oven to 350°. Use 2 Tbsp. butter to grease bottom and sides of a 9- x 5-inch loaf pan. Add 2 Tbsp. flour, and shake pan to evenly coat bottom and sides; tap out and discard any excess flour.

2. Sift together remaining 1¾ cups flour, cinnamon, baking soda, and salt in a large bowl. Peel bananas, and place in a small bowl; add lemon juice, and mash together, leaving some lumps of banana. Combine milk and sour cream and set aside.

3. Beat remaining 8 Tbsp. butter, sugars, and vanilla at low speed with an electric mixer until combined; increase speed to medium, and beat 1½ to 2 minutes or until fluffy. Add eggs, 1 at a time, beating well after each addition. Reduce speed to low, and add flour mixture alternately with milk mixture, beginning and ending with flour mixture. Beat just until blended after each addition. When dry ingredients are nearly incorporated, add banana mixture, beating no more than 10 seconds.

4. Spread batter in prepared loaf pan, and place on a baking sheet; bake 60 to 70 minutes or until a wooden pick inserted in center comes out clean. Cool in pan on a wire rack 10 minutes; run a knife around edges of loaf pan, and remove from pan to wire rack. Cool completely (about 50 minutes), and wrap in plastic wrap (it will still be warm, and wrapping it will help it stay moist); store up to 4 days.

CITRUS SHORTCAKES

Use any combination of your favorite citrus segments in this fresh shortcake spin. Just be sure to start with a total of 6 cups of fruit.

SERVES 8
HANDS-ON 20 min.
TOTAL 1 hr., 5 min.

SHORTCAKES

2	cups all-purpose flour
¼	cup granulated sugar
2	Tbsp. lemon zest
1	Tbsp. baking powder
¼	tsp. table salt
½	cup cold butter, cubed
1	cup plus 3 Tbsp. heavy cream, divided
½	tsp. lemon extract
	Parchment paper
1	large egg yolk
2	Tbsp. sparkling sugar

TOPPING

1½	cups heavy cream
¼	tsp. lemon extract
¾	cup powdered sugar
3	cups orange segments
3	cups red grapefruit segments
¼	cup torn fresh mint
¼	cup granulated sugar

1. Prepare Shortcakes: Preheat oven to 425°. Stir together first 5 ingredients in a large bowl. Cut butter into flour mixture with a pastry blender or fork until mixture resembles coarse meal. Make a well in center of mixture. Stir together 1 cup cream and ½ tsp. lemon extract. Add to dry ingredients, stirring just until dough comes together.

2. Turn dough out onto a lightly floured surface; knead lightly 2 to 3 times. Pat or roll dough to 1-inch thickness; cut into 8 rounds with a 2¼-inch round cutter. Place 2 inches apart on a parchment paper-lined baking sheet. Stir together egg yolk and remaining 3 Tbsp. cream; brush over tops of shortcakes. Sprinkle with sparkling sugar. Bake at 425° for 15 minutes or until golden. Cool completely (about 30 minutes).

3. Prepare Topping: Beat 1½ cups heavy cream and ¼ tsp. lemon extract at medium speed with an electric mixer until foamy. Gradually add powdered sugar, beating until soft peaks form.

4. Toss together oranges, grapefruit, mint, and ¼ cup granulated sugar. Split shortcakes in half lengthwise. Top bottom halves of shortcakes with half of fruit mixture and whipped cream. Cover with top halves of shortcakes, and top with remaining fruit mixture and whipped cream.

PECAN PIE BARS

MAKES 3 dozen
HANDS-ON 15 min.
TOTAL 3 hr., 15 min.

These bars have a very crisp, sugary crust, making them ideal to bake ahead.

Shortening

3   cups all-purpose flour
1   cup granulated sugar
¼   tsp. table salt
¾   cup cold butter, cut up
1½ cups light corn syrup
1   cup firmly packed light brown sugar
¼   cup butter
4   large eggs, lightly beaten
2½ cups coarsely chopped pecans
1   tsp. vanilla extract

1. Preheat oven to 350°. Grease a 15- x 10-inch jelly-roll pan with shortening. Whisk together flour, granulated sugar, and salt in a large bowl. Cut cold butter into flour mixture with a pastry blender or fork until crumbly. Press mixture into bottom of prepared pan. Bake for 17 to 20 minutes or until edges are light golden brown.

2. Combine corn syrup, brown sugar, and ¼ cup butter in a medium saucepan. Bring to a boil, whisking to dissolve sugar; cool 5 minutes. Whisk eggs in a large bowl. Gradually whisk half of hot syrup mixture into eggs; gradually whisk egg mixture into hot syrup mixture, whisking constantly. Stir in pecans and vanilla. Spread pecan mixture over crust. Bake at 350° for 20 minutes or until set. Cool completely on a wire rack (about 2 hours). Cut into 36 squares.

HONEY FLAN

Flans release like a dream if you let the custard cups stand in 1 inch of warm water for 3 to 5 minutes before unmolding.

½   cup sugar

7   Tbsp. honey (such as orange blossom), divided

1   (14-oz.) can sweetened condensed milk

1   cup milk

3   large eggs

1   large egg yolk

¼   tsp. kosher salt

1. Preheat oven to 350°. Sprinkle sugar in a 3-qt. saucepan; place over medium heat, and cook, gently shaking pan, 4 minutes or until sugar melts and turns a light golden brown. Slowly stir in 3 Tbsp. honey. (Mixture will clump a little; gently stir just until melted.) Remove from heat; immediately pour hot caramelized sugar into 6 (6-oz.) ramekins.

2. Process condensed milk, next 4 ingredients, and remaining 4 Tbsp. honey in a blender 10 to 15 seconds or until smooth; pour evenly over sugar in each ramekin. Place ramekins in a 13- x 9-inch pan. Add hot tap water to pan to a depth of 1 inch. Cover loosely with aluminum foil.

3. Bake at 350° for 30 to 35 minutes or until slightly set. (Flan will jiggle when pan is shaken.) Remove ramekins from water bath; place on a wire rack. Cool 30 minutes. Cover and chill 3 hours. Run a knife around edges of flans to loosen; invert flans onto a serving plate.

PEANUT BUTTER STREUSEL BROWNIES

Chocolate and peanut butter go hand-in-hand in these delightful bars. Don't skip lining the pan with foil—it makes the removal of the brownies a snap after baking.

MAKES 16 brownies
HANDS-ON 10 min.
TOTAL 2 hr.

4   (1-oz.) unsweetened chocolate baking squares
¾   cup butter
1½   cups granulated sugar
½   cup firmly packed brown sugar
3   large eggs
1   cup all-purpose flour
1   tsp. vanilla extract
¼   tsp. table salt, divided
½   cup all-purpose flour
2   Tbsp. light brown sugar
2   Tbsp. granulated sugar
⅓   cup chunky peanut butter
2   Tbsp. melted butter

1. Preheat oven to 350°. Line bottom and sides of an 8-inch pan with aluminum foil, allowing 2 to 3 inches to extend over sides; lightly grease foil.

2. Microwave chocolate squares and ¾ cup butter in a large microwave-safe bowl at HIGH 1½ to 2 minutes or until melted and smooth, stirring at 30-second intervals. Whisk in 1½ cups granulated and ½ cup brown sugar. Add eggs, 1 at a time, whisking just until blended after each addition. Whisk in 1 cup flour, vanilla, and ⅛ tsp. salt.

3. Pour mixture into prepared pan.

4. Stir together ½ cup flour, 2 Tbsp. brown sugar, 2 Tbsp. granulated sugar, peanut butter, 2 Tbsp. melted butter, and remaining ⅛ tsp. salt until blended and crumbly. Sprinkle peanut butter mixture over batter.

5. Bake at 350° for 50 to 54 minutes or until a wooden pick inserted in center comes out with a few moist crumbs. Cool completely on a wire rack (about 1 hour). Lift brownies from pan, using foil sides as handles. Gently remove foil, and cut brownies into 16 squares.

COCONUT CREAM PIE

SERVES 6 to 8
HANDS-ON 20 min.
TOTAL 1 hr., 20 min.

When it comes to pie recipes, this classic takes the blue ribbon! The use of a refrigerated piecrust makes it easy, and the whipped cream makes it stunning.

½ (15-oz.) package refrigerated piecrusts

½ cup sugar

¼ cup cornstarch

2 cups half-and-half

4 egg yolks

3 Tbsp. butter

1 cup sweetened flaked coconut

2½ tsp. vanilla extract, divided

2 cups whipping cream

⅓ cup sugar

1. Fit 1 piecrust into a 9-inch pie plate according to package directions; fold edges under, and crimp. Prick bottom and sides of piecrust with a fork. Bake according to package directions for a one-crust pie.

2. Combine ½ cup sugar and cornstarch in a heavy saucepan. Whisk together half-and-half and egg yolks. Gradually whisk egg mixture into sugar mixture; bring to a boil over medium heat, whisking constantly. Boil 1 minute; remove from heat.

3. Stir in butter, 1 cup coconut, and 1 tsp. vanilla. Place heavy-duty plastic wrap directly on warm custard in pan (to prevent a film from forming); let stand 30 minutes. Spoon custard mixture into prepared crust; cover and chill 30 minutes or until set.

4. Beat whipping cream at high speed with an electric mixer until foamy; gradually add ⅓ cup sugar and remaining 1½ tsp. vanilla, beating until soft peaks form. Spread or pipe whipped cream over pie filling. Garnish, if desired.

OOEY-CHEWY CHOCOLATE COOKIES

The title says just about all that needs to be said about this recipe. These cookies will be eaten in no time at all. They're pure chocolaty goodness. I adapted this recipe from a former baker of mine at Bayou Bakery—hats off to Becky!

MAKES 2 dozen
HANDS-ON 10 min.
TOTAL 22 min.

3¼ cups powdered sugar
1½ cups cocoa
½ tsp. kosher salt
2 cups semisweet chocolate morsels, melted
¾ cup egg whites, at room temperature (about 6 to 9 egg whites)
Parchment paper

1. Preheat oven to 375°. Combine powdered sugar, cocoa, and salt in a large bowl, and mix well. Slowly whisk in melted chocolate and egg whites, mixing just until combined (be careful not to overmix the dough—it should be sticky).

2. For each cookie, drop 3 Tbsp. dough on a parchment paper–lined baking sheet, leaving 2 inches of space between cookies; press dough into ½-inch disc. Bake 12 to 15 minutes or until edges are done and center is slightly underbaked.

DARK CHOCOLATE CHUNK COOKIES

MAKES 2 dozen
HANDS-ON 15 min.
TOTAL 50 min.

¾ cup uncooked regular oats
¼ cup butter, softened
¾ cup firmly packed light brown sugar
½ cup granulated sugar
2 large eggs
1 tsp. vanilla extract
1¾ cups all-purpose flour
½ tsp. baking soda
½ tsp. table salt
¼ tsp. baking powder
3 (4-oz.) bittersweet chocolate baking bars, coarsely chopped and divided
Parchment paper

1. Preheat oven to 400°. Bake oats in a 9-inch pie plate 10 to 12 minutes or until toasted and fragrant, stirring halfway through. Cool completely on a wire rack (about 30 minutes). Process oats in a blender or food processor 1 minute or until finely ground. Reduce oven temperature to 350°.

2. Beat butter and sugars at medium speed with a heavy-duty electric stand mixer until fluffy. Add eggs and vanilla, beating just until blended.

3. Stir together flour, next 3 ingredients, and ground oats in a small bowl; gradually add to butter mixture, beating just until blended after each addition. Fold in 2¼ cups chopped chocolate (about 2 bars) just until combined.

4. Drop dough by heaping tablespoonfuls onto parchment paper-lined baking sheets (about 6 per sheet).

5. Bake at 350° for 10 to 12 minutes or until golden brown; press remaining chocolate into cookies. Remove from baking sheets to wire racks; cool completely (about 15 minutes).

RED VELVET CUPCAKES

¾ cup butter, softened

1½ cups sugar

3 large eggs

1 (1-oz.) bottle red liquid food coloring

1 tsp. vanilla extract

2½ cups all-purpose flour

3 Tbsp. unsweetened cocoa

½ tsp. table salt

1 cup buttermilk

1 Tbsp. white vinegar

1 tsp. baking soda

White Chocolate-Amaretto Frosting

MAKES 2 dozen
HANDS-ON 25 min.
TOTAL 2 hr., 18 min.

1. Preheat oven to 350°. Beat butter at medium speed with an electric mixer until fluffy; gradually add sugar, beating well. Add eggs, 1 at a time, beating until blended. Stir in food coloring and vanilla until blended.

2. Combine flour, cocoa, and salt. Stir together buttermilk, vinegar, and baking soda in a 4-cup liquid measuring cup. Add flour mixture to butter mixture alternately with buttermilk mixture, beginning and ending with flour mixture. Beat at low speed until blended after each addition. Place 24 paper baking cups in 2 (12-cup) muffin pans; spoon batter into cups, filling three-fourths full.

3. Bake at 350° for 18 to 20 minutes or until wooden pick inserted in centers comes out clean. Remove cupcakes from pans to wire racks, and let cool completely. Pipe frosting onto cupcakes.

WHITE CHOCOLATE-AMARETTO FROSTING

Makes: 4 cups Hands-on: 20 min. Total: 50 min.

2 (4-oz.) white chocolate baking bars

⅓ cup heavy cream

1 cup butter, softened

6 cups powdered sugar

¼ cup almond liqueur

1. Break white chocolate baking bars into pieces. Cook white chocolate and cream in a microwave-safe bowl at MEDIUM (50% power) 1 minute or until melted and smooth, stirring at 30-second intervals. Let cool to room temperature. Beat butter and 1 cup powdered sugar at low speed with an electric mixer until blended. Add 5 cups powdered sugar alternately with almond liqueur, beating at low speed until blended after each addition. Add white chocolate mixture; beat at medium speed until spreading consistency.

BOURBON CHOCOLATE PUDDING WITH SALTED CARAMEL CREAM

MAKES 6 to 8
HANDS-ON 51 min.
TOTAL 51 min., plus 4 hr. for chilling

PUDDING

- 4 oz. bittersweet (70% cacao) chocolate, finely chopped
- 6 large egg yolks
- ½ cup granulated sugar
- 4 Tbsp. cornstarch
- 2 Tbsp. unsweetened Dutch process cocoa
- ¼ tsp. kosher salt
- 2 cups whole milk
- ¼ cup bourbon
- 1 tsp. vanilla extract
- 2 Tbsp. unsalted butter

CARAMEL CREAM

- 1 cup granulated sugar
- 2½ cups heavy cream, divided
- 1 Tbsp. superfine granulated sugar
- ½ tsp. kosher salt

1. Prepare Pudding: Place chocolate in a large bowl. Whisk together egg yolks, ½ cup sugar, cornstarch, cocoa, and salt in a medium bowl. Bring milk to a boil in a saucepan; remove from heat, and slowly whisk into egg mixture; transfer mixture back to saucepan. Place over medium-low heat, and cook, whisking constantly, 6 minutes or until thickened and glossy. Add bourbon and vanilla; immediately remove from heat. Strain custard through a fine wire-mesh strainer over chopped chocolate; stir until chocolate melts. Add butter; whisk gently until well mixed. Place heavy-duty plastic wrap directly on surface of pudding to prevent a film from forming; chill 4 hours.

2. Prepare Caramel Cream: Combine 1 cup granulated sugar and ¼ cup water in a 2-qt. saucepan; mix well. Place over medium-low heat; cover and cook, stirring occasionally, until sugar dissolves. Increase heat to medium-high, and bring mixture to a simmer; continue to cook until sugar turns light golden brown and begins to smoke. Remove from heat, and slowly add 1½ cups cream, being careful to avoid being burned by steam or splattering sugar. Place pan over medium-high heat, and quickly bring mixture to boil; remove from heat, and strain through a fine wire-mesh strainer. Cool completely.

3. Meanwhile, place a medium metal bowl in freezer for 10 minutes. Place superfine granulated sugar into chilled bowl, and add remaining 1 cup cream; whisk until medium to stiff peaks form. Fold in caramel cream and kosher salt, swirling it into the sugar-cream mixture. Before serving, whisk pudding 15 seconds or until soft and smooth; spoon evenly into 6 to 8 custard cups or rocks glasses. Top each serving with a dollop of caramel cream.

LEMONY-LIMEY ICE BOX PIE

SERVES 8

HANDS-ON 25 min.

TOTAL 1 hr., 25 min., plus 6 hr. for freezing

14 graham crackers

¼ cup sugar

¼ tsp. table salt

6 Tbsp. unsalted butter, melted and still warm

2 (14-oz. cans) sweetened condensed milk

½ cup plus 2 Tbsp. fresh lemon juice

½ cup plus 2 Tbsp. fresh lime juice

1 Tbsp. lemon zest

1 Tbsp. lime zest

8 egg yolks

Garnishes: lemon and lime zest

1. Preheat oven to 325°. Break the graham crackers into small pieces, and place in bowl of a food processor; add sugar and salt. Pulse 8 times, or until the cracker crumbs are semi-fine and the crackers and sugar are combined. Pour in the butter and pulse until the butter is blended in and the mixture holds its shape when you squeeze it (about 12 [1-second] pulses). Press on bottom and two-thirds up sides of a 9-inch springform pan. Set aside.

2. Whisk together condensed milk, lemon juice, and lime juice; set aside. Whisk together lemon zest, lime zest, and egg yolks in a medium bowl until pale, 30 to 60 seconds. Whisk condensed milk mixture into egg mixture until combined.

3. Place the springform pan on a rimmed baking sheet, and pour the egg mixture into the crust. Carefully transfer the baking sheet to the oven. Bake at 325° about 25 minutes or until the center is almost set. Remove from oven, and place on a wire rack. Cool for 1 hour. Loosely cover with plastic wrap, making sure plastic wrap does not touch the top of the pie. Freeze for at least 6 hours or overnight.

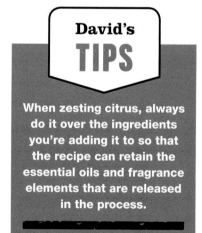

David's
TIPS

When zesting citrus, always do it over the ingredients you're adding it to so that the recipe can retain the essential oils and fragrance elements that are released in the process.

ROCKY ROAD ICE-CREAM CAKE

Layered with brownies and chock-full of nuts, marshmallows, and fudge topping, this chocolate lover's dream would make the perfect ice-cream birthday cake.

SERVES 10
HANDS-ON 15 min.
TOTAL 1 hr., 33 min., plus 8 hr. for freezing

Vegetable cooking spray

1 (18.75-oz.) package premium brownie mix

⅓ cup vegetable oil

1 large egg

1 cup miniature marshmallows

1 cup walnuts halves, chopped

½ cup semisweet chocolate mini-morsels

½ cup hot fudge topping

4 cups rocky road ice cream, softened

Garnishes: chopped walnuts, miniature marshmallows, and semisweet chocolate mini-morsels

1. Preheat oven to 325°. Line bottom and sides of a 13- x 9-inch pan with aluminum foil, allowing 2 to 3 inches to extend over 2 long sides of pan; lightly grease foil with cooking spray.

2. Stir together brownie mix, oil, egg, and ¼ cup water in a medium bowl; spread batter in prepared pan.

3. Bake at 325° for 15 to 18 minutes or until a wooden pick inserted in center comes out with a few moist crumbs. Cool completely in pan on a wire rack (about 1 hour). Lift brownies from pan, using foil sides as handles. Cut crosswise into thirds; carefully remove foil.

4. Line bottom and sides of a 9- x 5-inch loaf pan with 2 layers of plastic wrap, allowing 3 inches to extend over all sides. Stir together marshmallows, walnuts, and mini-morsels in a medium bowl. Spoon fudge topping into a zip-top plastic freezer bag; snip 1 corner of bag to make a hole about ¼ inch in diameter.

5. Place one-third of brownies in bottom of prepared loaf pan, and sprinkle with half of marshmallow mixture; drizzle with half of fudge topping, and dollop with half of softened ice cream, spreading gently. Repeat layers once, and top with remaining one-third of brownie. Wrap with plastic overhang; freeze 8 hours or until firm.

6. Lift cake from pan, using plastic wrap as handles. Unwrap cake, and cut crosswise into 10 slices.

CARAMELIZED FIG ICE CREAM

MAKES about 1 qt.

HANDS-ON 1 hr., 27 min.

TOTAL 1 hr., 57 min., plus 20 hr. for chilling

This decadent ice cream is a great way to use summer's harvest of fresh figs. If you have any leftovers, quarter them and serve them on top, along with a drizzle of honey.

1½ cups sugar, divided
1 lb. fresh figs, stemmed and chopped
1½ tsp. orange zest
1 Tbsp. fresh orange juice
2 Tbsp. butter
3 cups half-and-half
3 large egg yolks
2 tsp. vanilla extract

1. Combine ½ cup sugar and ¼ cup water in a large heavy saucepan; cook over medium heat 6 to 8 minutes or until sugar melts and turns a light golden brown, tipping pan to incorporate mixture. Stir in figs, zest, and juice; cook 5 to 6 minutes or until mixture is bubbly and figs start to break down, stirring occasionally.

2. Remove from heat; stir in butter. Cool completely (about 1 hour). Cover and chill 8 to 24 hours.

3. Whisk together remaining 1 cup sugar, half-and-half, and egg yolks in a large heavy saucepan. Cook over medium heat, whisking constantly, 8 to 10 minutes or until mixture slightly thickens. Pour into a large bowl; whisk in vanilla. Cool completely (about 1 hour), stirring occasionally. Place plastic wrap directly on warm custard (to prevent a film from forming), and chill 8 to 24 hours.

4. Gently stir caramelized fig mixture into half-and-half mixture. Pour mixture into freezer container of a 2-qt. electric ice-cream maker, and freeze according to manufacturer's instructions (instructions and times may vary). Freeze in an airtight container at least 4 hours before serving.

STRAWBERRY ICE-CREAM SANDWICHES

MAKES 6 sandwiches

HANDS-ON 10 min.

TOTAL 10 min., plus 2 hr. for freezing

If ice cream starts to melt while assembling these treats, keep sandwiches in freezer while working, and remove only one at a time to fill.

⅓ cup chopped fresh strawberries

2 Tbsp. strawberry preserves

12 devil's food cookie cakes

2 Tbsp. hot fudge topping

¾ cup strawberry ice cream

1. In small bowl, gently stir strawberries and preserves.

2. Place cookies, flat sides up, on work surface. Top each of 6 cookies with 1 tsp. fudge topping. Top each of remaining 6 cookies with 1 heaping Tbsp. strawberry mixture and 2 Tbsp. ice cream. Place fudge-topped cookies, fudge side down, on ice cream; gently press together.

3. Place in plastic or wax paper sandwich bags. Freeze at least 2 hours or until firm.

TEMPERATURE GUIDE

Use the following grilling methods and times whenever you step up to the grill.

Beef and Game

CUT	HEAT	TIME
STEAK (rib-eye, T-bone, filet mignon, New York Strip) 1 inch thick	Direct high heat	8 to 10 minutes
GROUND BEEF	Direct high heat	8 to 10 minutes
FLANK STEAK	Direct medium heat	8 to 10 minutes
RIB ROAST (boneless) 5 to 6 pounds	Indirect medium heat	1 to 2 hours
TRI-TIP 2 to 2½ pounds	Indirect medium heat	30 to 40 minutes
VEAL LOIN CHOP	Direct high heat	6 to 8 minutes
LAMB CHOP	Direct medium heat	8 to 12 minutes

Pork

CUT	HEAT	TIME
BRATWURST	Direct medium heat	10 to 12 minutes
CHOP 1 inch thick	Direct medium heat	8 to 10 minutes
LOIN (boneless) 2½ pounds	Direct medium heat	40 to 50 minutes
SHOULDER 5 to 6 pounds	Indirect low heat	5 to 7 hours
RIBS (baby back) 1½ to 2 pounds	Indirect low heat	3 to 4 hours
TENDERLOIN 1 pound	Direct medium heat	15 to 20 minutes

Poultry

CUT	HEAT	TIME
BREAST (bone-in)	Direct medium heat Indirect medium heat	3 to 5 minutes 20 to 30 minutes
BREAST (boneless)	Direct medium heat	8 to 12 minutes
THIGH (bone-in)	Direct medium heat Indirect medium heat	6 to 10 minutes 30 minutes
WHOLE 4 to 5 pound	Indirect medium heat	1 to 1¼ hours
WINGS	Direct medium heat Indirect medium heat	5 to 8 minutes 30 minutes
TURKEY (whole) 10 to 12 pounds	Indirect low heat	2½ to 3½ hours

Fish and Shellfish

TYPE	HEAT	TIME
FILLET 1 inch thick	Direct high heat	3 to 5 minutes
WHOLE FISH 2 pounds	Indirect medium heat	20 to 30 minutes
CLAMS	Direct high heat	6 to 8 minutes
OYSTERS	Direct high heat	2 to 4 minutes
SCALLOPS	Direct high heat	4 to 6 minutes
SHRIMP	Direct high heat	2 to 4 minutes

METRIC EQUIVALENTS

The information in the following charts is provided to help cooks outside the United States successfully use the recipes in this book. All equivalents are approximate.

Equivalents for Different Types of Ingredients

Standard Cup	Fine Powder (ex. flour)	Grain (ex. rice)	Granular (ex. sugar)	Liquid Solids (ex. butter)	Liquid (ex. milk)
1	140 g	150 g	190 g	200 g	240 ml
¾	105 g	113 g	143 g	150 g	180 ml
⅔	93 g	100 g	125 g	133 g	160 ml
½	70 g	75 g	95 g	100 g	120 ml
⅓	47 g	50 g	63 g	67 g	80 ml
¼	35 g	38 g	48 g	50 g	60 ml
⅛	18 g	19 g	24 g	25 g	30 ml

Dry Ingredients by Weight

(To convert ounces to grams, multiply the number of ounces by 30.)

1 oz	=	¹/₁₆ lb	=	30 g
4 oz	=	¼ lb	=	120 g
8 oz	=	½ lb	=	240 g
12 oz	=	¾ lb	=	360 g
16 oz	=	1 lb	=	480 g

Length

(To convert inches to centimeters, multiply the number of inches by 2.5.)

1 in				=	2.5 cm		
6 in	=	½ ft	=		15 cm		
12 in	=	1 ft	=		30 cm		
36 in	=	3 ft	=	1 yd	=	90 cm	
40 in				=	100 cm	=	1 m

Liquid Ingredients by Volume

¼ tsp	=					1 ml	
½ tsp	=					2 ml	
1 tsp	=					5 ml	
3 tsp	=	1 Tbsp	=		½ fl oz	=	15 ml
		2 Tbsp	=	⅛ cup	=	1 fl oz	=	30 ml
		4 Tbsp	=	¼ cup	=	2 fl oz	=	60 ml
		5⅓ Tbsp	=	⅓ cup	=	3 fl oz	=	80 ml
		8 Tbsp	=	½ cup	=	4 fl oz	=	120 ml
		10⅔ Tbsp	=	⅔ cup	=	5 fl oz	=	160 ml
		12 Tbsp	=	¾ cup	=	6 fl oz	=	180 ml
		16 Tbsp	=	1 cup	=	8 fl oz	=	240 ml
		1 pt	=	2 cups	=	16 fl oz	=	480 ml
		1 qt	=	4 cups	=	32 fl oz	=	960 ml
					33 fl oz	=	1000 ml	=	1 L

Cooking/Oven Temperatures

	Farenheit	Celsius	Gas Mark
Freeze Water	32°F	0°C	
Room Temperature	68°F	20°C	
Boil Water	212°F	100°C	
Bake	325°F	160°C	3
	350°F	180°C	4
	375°F	190°C	5
	400°F	200°C	6
	425°F	220°C	7
	450°F	230°C	8
Broil			Grill

INDEX

ISBN-13: 978-0-8487-4638-4
ISBN-10: 0-8487-4638-4
Library of Congress Control Number: 2015932677

Printed in the United States of America
First Printing 2015

Oxmoor House

Creative Director: Felicity Keane
Art Director: Christopher Rhoads
Executive Photography Director: Iain Bagwell
Executive Food Director: Grace Parisi
Managing Editor: Elizabeth Tyler Austin
Assistant Managing Editor: Jeanne de Lathouder

Grill Nation

Associate Editor: Meredith L. Butcher
Project Editor: Emily Chappell Connolly
Editorial Assistant: April Smitherman
Assistant Designer: Allison Sperando Potter
Assistant Test Kitchen Manager:
    Alyson Moreland Haynes
Recipe Developers and Testers: Stefanie Maloney,
    Callie Nash, Karen Rankin
Food Stylists: Nathan Carrabba, Victoria E. Cox,
    Margaret Monroe Dickey,
    Catherine Crowell Steele
Photo Editor: Kellie Lindsey
Senior Photographer: Hélène Dujardin
Senior Photo Stylists: Kay E. Clarke,
    Mindi Shapiro Levine
Senior Production Manager: Sue Chodakiewicz
Production Manager: Theresa Beste-Farley

Contributors

Author: David Guas
Designer: Nancy Leonard
Copy Editors: Norma Butterworth-McKittrick,
    Polly Linthicum
Proofreaders: Cathy Fowler, Rebecca Henderson
Indexer: Mary Ann Laurens
Fellows: Laura Arnold, Kylie Dazzo, Nicole Fisher,
    Loren Lorenzo, Anna Ramia, Caroline Smith,
    Amanda Widis
Photographers: Johnny Autry, Hector Sanchez (front cover)
Food and Photo Stylist: Charlotte Autry

Time Home Entertainment Inc.

Publisher: Margot Schupf
Vice President, Finance: Vandana Patel
Executive Director, Marketing Services:
    Carol Pittard
Publishing Director: Megan Pearlman
Assistant General Counsel: Simone Procas